Issues in Money and Banking

Issues in Money and Banking

George Macesich

Westport, Connecticut
London

Library of Congress Cataloging-in-Publication Data

Macesich, George, 1927–
    Issues in money and banking / George Macesich.
      p. cm.
    Includes bibliographical references and index.
    ISBN 0–275–96777–8 (alk. paper)
    1. Money. 2. Banks and banking. I. Title.
HG221.M122 2000
332.1—dc21   99–055877

British Library Cataloguing in Publication Data is available.

Library of Congress Catalog Card Number: 99–055877
ISBN: 0–275–96777–8

First published in 2000

Praeger Publishers, 88 Post Road West, Westport, CT 06881
An imprint of Greenwood Publishing Group, Inc.
www.praeger.com

Printed in the United States of America

∞™

The paper used in this book complies with the
Permanent Paper Standard issued by the National
Information Standards Organization (Z39.48–1984).

10 9 8 7 6 5 4 3 2 1

For
Carol, Walter,
and
family

Contents

Preface

The purpose of this book is to cast into perspective the ongoing changes in money and banking. In order to draw on a wider audience, the study restricts itself as much as possible to nontechnical language, although on a number of issues such language is difficult to avoid. It is important, after all, that people, other than specialists, have more than a nodding acquaintance with issues that have profound implications for both the domestic and world economy.

The issues discussed in this study are long-standing. Some have their antecedents in distant history and others are more recent. They are all tied by society's use of money. There is, moreover, no guarantee that these issues in money and banking will follow a given script. For instance, financial institutions are rushing to meet the challenges of Europe's new "euro" currency. The world's big banks are confident that they can greet the euro without undue strains on their activities. More worried are small- and middle-sized banks, which are generally less prepared to deal with new developments on the world's financial scene.

Most American banks' profits continue to come from lending. Many banks have also become exposed to lesser borrowers; as a result they are likely to suffer bad credit losses. Another likely source of trouble for banks is that some of the businesses they entered, such as asset management and trading, may well become much less attractive.

In Europe and Asia too banks are at risk. The pressures on banks to earn more profits and the extra risk they have taken to achieve them merit a review of the key issues raised in this study. Indeed, the world's banking systems, from the prosperous American economy to muddled Europe to wobbly Japan, may well be in worse shape than is usually assumed.

I am grateful to Karen Wells for preparing this manuscript for publication.

Chapter 1

Money

WHAT IS MONEY?

Money is a medium of exchange as well as a store of value. It solves the critical problem of the "dual coincidence of barter." That is, X must have to exchange for what the other person "Y" has and Y must have what X wants. Since both X and Y widely accept M; the problem is solved. Money, M, in whatever form or shape it takes in a given period in history, must foremost possess the characteristic that it is acceptable to the public at large for the exchange of goods and services.

Historically, various commodities and items have served, and indeed some still serve, as money. The better known are gold, copper, and silver. Others, though lesser known, are iron, cattle, beads, tobacco, and stone.[1] Today money includes currency, bank deposits payable on demand and transferable by check, as well as other liquid assets that are regularly compiled by a country's monetary authorities and serve as the empirical counterpart of money.[2]

Clearly, it is difficult to say how a commodity or something else becomes generally accepted by the public as money. Certainly habit in the use of a given item or commodity as money is important. It is thus more than likely that a generally accepted commodity achieves the status of money through evolution rather than imposition. As such, it serves the important functions of money, such as general acceptance for exchange of goods and services and as a temporary abode of purchasing powers.

Considerable confusion arose over the value of money when it consisted primarily of gold and silver. It was regularly insisted that money must have the support of gold and silver if indeed it was to be taken seriously as money. This suggests, in effect, that gold or silver cover of money is the source of the exchange value or purchasing power of money and so quite independent of its monetary role. This is the so-called metallist fallacy.[3] Once gold and silver, for instance, acquired the status of money, other factors influenced their exchange value. The (nonmonetary) value of a commodity is never a fixed magnitude. It depends on tastes and preferences and on relative quantities.[4] Indeed Friedman discusses one such episode in American history in 1873 and the effect of the demonetization of silver.[5] The episode illustrates how the nonmonetary demand for an item used as money has an important effect on its monetary value while at the same time the monetary demand affects its nonmonetary value.

Indeed, the current worldwide fiat monetary regime uses pure paper money that has little value as a commodity.[6] To be sure this is an unprecedented development. In the past paper money was the exception rather than the general rule. It was expected that any use of paper money was temporary and that the link with the monetary metal would be restored as quickly as possible. All this came to an end on August 15, 1971, when President Richard M. Nixon "closed the gold window" ending the obligation the United States had assumed at Bretton Woods to convert dollars held by foreign monetary authorities into gold at the fixed price of $35 an ounce. Nevertheless, many central banks the world over continue to carry gold on their backs.

How is the value of money, that is, in terms of the value of good and services, established? As with any other commodity or service this is established by supply and demand, and in this instance, by the supply and demand for money. This study discusses how, in fact, the supply of money and the demand for money are determined. Before these issues are taken up, however, it is important to underscore important philosophical differences held by analysts on the role of money in society. These differences are perhaps best illustrated by the views of monetarists, Austrians, and Keynesians.

MONETARISTS, AUSTRIANS, KEYNESIANS AND MONEY

Milton Friedman identifies "monetarism" with the quantity theory of money, suggesting thereby that monetarism is not a new development.[7] The principle tenet of monetarism, as in the quantity theory of money, is that inflation is at all times and everywhere a monetary phenomenon. Its principle policy corollary is that only a slow and steady rate of increase in the money—one in line with the real growth of the economy—can ensure price stability.

Milton Friedman summarizes the monetarist view on the relationship between the money supply and the price level in the following:

1. There is a consistent, though not precise, relation between the rate of growth of the quantity of money and the rate of growth of nominal income;
2. This relationship is not obvious to the naked eye, largely because it takes time for changes in monetary growth to affect income. How long this process will take is within itself a variable;
3. On average, a change in the rate of monetary growth produces a change in the rate of growth of nominal income about six to nine months later. This is an average that does not hold in every individual case;
4. The changed rate of growth in nominal income typically shows up first in output and hardly at all in prices;
5. On average, the effect on prices comes about six to nine months after the effect on income and output, so the total delay between a change in monetary growth and a change in the rate of inflation averages around twelve to eighteen months;
6. Even after allowances for delays in the effect of monetary growth the relation is far from perfect, for there are many a slip "twixt the monetary change and the income change";
7. In the short-run, which may be as much as five or ten years, monetary changes primarily affect output over decades, although the rate of monetary growth affects prices primarily.[8]

The monetarist view, as summarized here by Friedman, in effect questions the doctrine advanced by Keynes that variations in government spending, taxes, and the national debt could stabilize both the price level and the real economy. This doctrine has come to be called The Keynesian Revolution.

· It is to the Austrian school of thought and through such members as Carl von Menger, Georg Simmel (actually a sociologist), Ludwig von Mises, Friedrich Hayek, and their followers that useful insights into money and the monetary system have become an integral part of the social structure. These views differ significantly from both Keynesian and monetarist views, though Milton Friedman and some monetarists come closer to the Austrians in their emphasis on "monetary rules" and a stable monetary order.

According to the Austrian view, money and the monetary system are the unintended products of social evolution in much the same fashion as the legal system. Money is a social institution—a public good. It is not simply another durable good held in the form of "real balances" by utility maximizing firms as Keynesian and monetarist views hold. However useful the tools of demand and supply analysis are when applied to money as a private durable good, Keynesians and monetarists miss the full effect of monetary instability.

In essence, money and the monetary system are integral parts of the social fabric whose threads include faith and trust, which make possible the exercise of rational choice and the development of human freedom. This is misunderstood by the very people who benefit from it. It is this misunderstanding of the social role of money as a critical element in the market mechanism and the need for confidence in the stability of its purchasing power that came to dominate much of Keynesian and monetarist thought in the post-war period. This misunderstanding is the ideological key to the use of discretionary monetary policies for monetary expansion as an unfailing means of increasing output and employment and reducing interest rates.

Herbert Frankel writes that Keynes, following Georg Friedrich Knapp, presents money and the monetary system as a creation of the state and as such available for manipulation by government consisting mostly of wise and well-educated people disinterestedly promoting the best interests of society.[8] The fact that such an arrangement, argues Frankel, curtails individual choice and decision did not disturb Keynes who saw little reason to believe that those choices and decisions benefit society. In essence, it is at best an elitist view of government so familiar to Great Britain at the turn of the twentieth century or at worst a totalitarian government similar to that of the former Soviet Union. David Laidler takes exception to Frankel's argument that Keynes is the architect of a short-run monetary policy that seeks to exploit monetary illusion in order to trick people into taking actions that, if they could correctly foresee their consequences, they would not take. Such "trickery" is not the policy of the 1930s when Keynes believed that undertaking an activist monetary policy to deal with unemployment would be what individual agents desired but were prevented from accomplishing on their own because of price and market mechanism failures. Keynes, in effect, thought he was dealing with the issue of involuntary unemployment. It was in the 1950s and 1960s that the idea of a stable inflation-unemployment trade-off generated a "money illusion" available for exploitation by policymakers.

In drawing on Georg Simmel's view for a free and stable monetary order, Frankel does not take into sufficient account the political environment in which Keynes and his followers worked. As a result, he attributes too much responsibility to Keynes and his followers for the lack of faith and trust in the "old order." The free monetary order that underpinned Simmel's turn-of-the-century society can be defended on moral grounds as "an ideal—the pursuit of trust." The durability of the old order was questioned by Simmel, as Frankel points out, long before Keynes and his followers appeared.[9]

Its durability is questioned by Simmel throughout his *Philosophy of Money*.[10] His concern is not simply with money as a unit of account, a store of value, and medium of exchange, but with the free market, in which money and the monetary system are integral parts, and the relationship between institutions of such an economy and the matters of justice, liberty, and the nature of man as a social being. The focus is on exchange as one of the most fundamental functions that serves to tie individuals into a cohesive social group.

Since barter exchange is inconvenient, a group of individuals naturally developed who specialized in exchange and the institution of money, which serves to solve the problem of the dual coincidence of barter. As soon as money enters the picture and the dual coincidence of barter is resolved, exchange ceases to be a simple relationship between two individuals. Simmel notes that the ensuing generalization of claims made possible by money transfers places these claims for realization upon the general economic community and government as its representative.

Unlike other things that have a specific content from which they derive their value, money derives its content, according to Simmel, from its value. Its value in turn owes much to the implicit guarantee given by society and the community and little to the physical properties of money. It is, in effect, based on the confidence in the sociopolitical organization and order. In this view, the British pound sterling, formerly, and the American dollar, currently, owe their value more to the political and economic power and prestige of their institutions than to the physical properties of the pound and dollar. This confidence in the political and economic institutions of a country, which Laidler, Rowe, and Frankel attribute to Simmel (in translation), is "trust."

Trust then is the cement of society and the more of it individuals have in a society's institutions in general and in its money in particular the more extension and depth of use of money will occur in an economy. By and large the consequences of such developments are beneficial to society in that man's achievements are enhanced not only in the economy but in all other endeavors. Indeed, freedom and justice are promoted by the development and growth of exchange and the monetary economy. As a consequence, the individual is enabled to act independently of other individuals while at the same time become more dependent on society as a whole. That is, an individual becomes more dependent on the achievements of individuals and less so on the peculiarities of personalities. The loosening of bonds serves to promote economic freedom, which may or may not promote political freedom at the same time.

Simmel underscores two likely sources of trouble for a free monetary order, which are serious enough to threaten the survival of the order. First, the receipt of money wages instead of payment in kind while promoting individual freedom exposes the recipient to the uncertainties and fluctuations of the market, originating in turn in fluctuations in the purchasing power of money. Second, the very success of the free monetary order also encourages the development of socialist ideas, which serve to undermine Simmel's concern about fluctuations in general and inflation in particular since the uncertainty so generated undermines trust in the monetary order.[11]

In fact, Laidler's evaluation of the significance of the "Austrian" view of money is basically correct. If money is taken to be one among a complex of social institutions, one consequence of inflation is to move the social order away from the use of money and toward a greater reliance on more government control in various forms or command organizations. Such development, Laidler notes, increases the dependence of individuals on other "specific personalities" and less on freedom—so much for anticipated inflation.[12]

In an unanticipated inflation, the Austrian view foresees an increase in uncertainty inherent in a monetary economy that could undermine mutual trust which is essential for monetary exchange. The net effect would be a decline in the number of mutually beneficial exchanges taking place. Since monetary instability and market failure are closely linked in the Austrian view, both anticipated and unanticipated inflation serve to weaken the social fabric.

As Laidler and Rowe state:

if monetary theory is best approached along Austrian lines, then we must conclude that mainstream monetary theory, for all its considerable accomplishments, not only trivializes the social consequences of inflation in particular . . . but that it grossly underestimates the destructiveness of monetary instability in general. . . Note that we will refer to modern monetary theory and not to its proponents. The principal authors of the "shoe leather" approach to analyzing the cost of inflation, such as Friedman, have expressed far more concern about the importance of controlling or avoiding inflation than their theories could possible justify, as their opponents [e.g., James Tobin, "Inflation Control as a Social Priority," 1977, cited by Laidler and Row] have been quick to point out. In this their instincts have, in our view, run far ahead of their analysis.[13]

According to Laidler and Rowe, Keynes, too was concerned with monetary stability and the fragile nature of a money-using market economy and the social order that went with it. He was also well aware of the need for "trust" in the stability of purchasing power if the market mechanism was to function properly. Indeed, to Keynes money is not just another commodity. A money economy is very different from a barter economy. This idea was lost, write Laidler and Rowe, "as the Hicksian IS-LM (Investment/Saving-Liquidity/Money) interpretation of the *General Theory* came to dominate monetary economics—'monetarist' as well as so-called 'Keynesian.' The dominance of this complete version of Keynes in subsequent debates has surely been the main reason for participants in them leaving neglected 'Austrian' ideas on these matters."[14]

The story, however, is very different on the conduct of monetary policy where Keynes and his followers depart significantly from the Austrian and monetarist paths. These differences are so profound they overwhelm areas of agreement. Keynes believed firmly in discretionary monetary policy and viewed the gold standard as a relic. Modern Austrians hold to the gold standard as an important means for constraining government and discretionary policy. The monetarists argue for a given growth in the stock of money. The difference between the Austrians and the monetarists is essentially about the means to achieve agreed upon ends, though the latter do not stress the role of stability in promoting trust and so facilitating the functioning of markets. The Austrians, while distrusting the bureaucrats, are more skeptical than monetarists about the stability of the demand for money function, and they argue for pegging the price of money in terms of gold relying on the stability of the relative price of gold in terms of goods in general.

Frankel, in his study *Two Philosophies of Money*, directs attention to the erroneous "nominalist" theories of money that imply that money is something external to the fabric of society, a thing or commodity in its own right that governments are entitled to manipulate in pursuit of their own limited economic or social ends. He draws and compares the views of Simmel and Keynes, arguing that both understood the economic uses and psychological power of money. Simmel and Keynes were also sensitive to its resultant influence on human character and behavior. More important perhaps, Frankel demonstrates how the views of Simmel and Keynes summarize the conflicting ideologies of the nineteenth and twentieth centuries and serve to place in perspective contemporary monetary problems. According to Frankel, "It arises out of the conflict between money as a *tool* of state action and money as a *symbol* of social trust. The two concepts are incompatible. I go so far as to contend that for several decades we have been witnessing an intense reaction against traditional concepts of monetary order: it is not far removed from a revolt against it."[15]

The traditional view of money focused on a free market order "implies the possibility for individuals of choosing between a multiplicity of conflicting goals or ends. It postulates the existence of principles, enforced by customs, convention and law, which ensure that its operation will not be arbitrarily, capricious, or lightly altered in favor of particular groups, individuals, or interest."[16] The real nature of the monetary debate, argues Frankel, "is basically not about inflation or deflation, fixed or flexible exchange rate, gold or paper standards and so forth, it is about the kind of society in which money is to operate."[17]

The survival of the free monetary order is questioned because it might not prove possible to make it work in terms of specific goals that society should, in their opinion, pursue. This view, shared by Keynes, leads to utopian attempts to make the uncertain certain by control of society according to plan as well as by transformation of man.[18] This is reflected, writes Frankel, in the ongoing highly sophisticated debate about the scope, legitimacy, and effectiveness of monetary policy. On one hand, there are the optimists who believe that we now possess the technical tools and scientific knowledge to enable us to control monetary behavior, not only within a nation, but even internationally and thereby not only the rate of economic change, but progress also. On the other hand, their opponents would support Friedman's view that "We are in danger of asking it to accomplish tasks that it cannot achieve and, as a result, in danger of preventing it from making the contribution that it is capable of making."[19]

To use the monetary system to pursue changing goals and objectives is incompatible with monetary order, argues Frankel. It will make it "capricious and uncertain and prey to conflicting and varying political objectives."[20] Intended to reduce uncertainty, monetary manipulation actually increases it by casting in doubt the monetary system itself. A monetary policy, writes Frankel, "which is directed to shifting goals . . . as for example, full employment, economic growth, economic equality or the attempt to satisfy conflicting demands of capital and labour . . . cannot but vary with the goals adopted."[21]

According to Frankel, it is Keynes who made the revolt against the predominant nineteenth-century view of money respectable. It was Georg Simmel—especially in *The Philosophy of Money*, first published in 1907 in Berlin—who first suggested the causes of the revolt and foresaw their likely consequences. In essence, Simmel does not see the institution of money in neoclassical terms but, as Frankel writes, "a conflict between our abstract conception of money and the social trust on which it rests. He was concerned to elucidate the moral basis of monetary order in contrast to the subversion of morals through money, in the abstract which he feared."[22]

The nineteenth-century view of society's responsibility to maintain trust and faith in money was supported by the bitter eighteenth-century experiences with paper currency excesses. Most classical economists and certainly the "Austrians" underscored society's monetary responsibilities for preserving trust and faith in money. Simmel's contributions to monetary thought are in keeping with the spirit of the tradition. Simmel is against the use of discretionary monetary policy for the purpose of exploiting the presumed short-run nonneutrality of money in order to increase permanent employment and output by increasing the stock of money. Though an arbitrary increase in money, according to Simmel, will not necessarily disrupt relative prices permanently, such manipulation sets into motion forces whose consequences for social stability are very serious indeed. Since no human power can guarantee against possible misuse of the money issuing authority, to give such authority to government is to invite destruction of the social order. To avoid such temptation, it is best to tie paper money to a metal value established by law or the economy.[23]

Of course, Keynes, too, was essentially a monetary economist. His writings are an integral part of our received monetary heritage. Certainly his work, *Monetary Reform*, draws on this heritage while at the same time adds to it.[24] It was also Keynes who in 1919 in his *Economic Consequences of the Peace* stated that there is no better means to overturn an existing social structure than to debauch the currency.[25] He also alleged that Lenin indeed espoused that the best way to overthrow the capitalist system was to debauch the currency. Ironically, some can argue that it was also Keynes' subsequent teaching that opened the floodgates of inflation in the post–World War II period, even though he personally attempted to close these shortly before his death in 1946.[26]

Keynes clearly shared a monetary heritage common to Simmel, the Austrians, and the monetarists. What sets him apart, of course, are his views on the conduct of monetary policy. Friedman, for instance, writes that his point of disagreement with the views Keynes expressed in monetary reform is with the appropriate method for achieving a stable price level.[27] Keynes favored managed money and managed exchange rates—that is, discretionary control by monetary authorities.[28]

It appears that it is the exercise of discretionary policy by monetary authorities advocated by Keynes that underscores his differences with the monetarists and Austrians. Setting aside the monetary role of gold as a barbarous relic casts him in disagreement with the Austrians. His desire to place the execution of monetary policy at the discretion of public-spirited and competent civil servants sets him in disagreement with monetarists who argue for growth-rate rule for some definitions of the money supply. But some of these differences cast Keynes out of our received monetary heritage.[29]

Keynes' preference for discretionary monetary policy as exercised by our enlightened elite, in part, can be rationalized by an appeal to monetary nominalism, chartism, or better, state money. To begin with, Keynes writes that the "currency-of-account" is the primary concept of the theory of money, in effect, paper money can exist only in relation to a "currency-of-account."[30] He argues that money-of-account is the description or title, and "money" is the thing that answers that description.[31] If the same thing is always answered to the same description, writes Keynes, the distinction would have no practical interest.[32] On the other hand, if the thing that is called money can change while its description remains the same, the distinction can indeed be significant.

As for contracts and promises to deliver goods and services in the future, custom or law serves as the basis for their enforcement, according to Keynes. At this point, the state or community is introduced, for it is they who enforce delivery, "but also which decides what it is that must be delivered as lawful or customary discharge of a contract which has been concluded in terms of money of account."[33] The state, therefore, is also an authority of law that corresponds to the name or description in the contract. The State comes in first of all as an authority of law which enforces payment of the thing which corresponds to the name or description in the contract. But it comes in doubly when, in addition, "it claims the right to determine and declare <u>what thing</u> corresponds to the name, and to vary its declaration from time to time—when, it claims the right to re-edit the dictionary. This right is claimed by all modern states and has been so claimed by some four thousand years at least. It is when this stage in the evolution of money has been reached that Knapp's chartalism—the doctrine that money is peculiarly a creation of the state—is fully realized."[34]

In Keynes' view, all money is chartist or state money. Bank money, for its part, is simply an acknowledgment of private debt expressed in the money-of-account used alongside or alternatively with money paper to settle a transaction. He includes in the *Treatise on Money* as state money, not only that which is compulsory legal tender but also money that the state or the central bank undertakes to accept in payments to itself or to exchange for compulsory legal-tender money.

Managed money, according to Keynes, is the most generalized form of money. This type of money can be "considered to degenerate with commodity money on the one side when the managing authority holds against it a hundred percent of the objective standard, so that it is in effect a warehouse warrant, and into fiat money on the other side when it loses its objective standard. Keynes argues that "chartelism begins when the state <u>designates</u> the objective standard which shall correspond to the money-of-account. Representative money begins when money is no longer composed of its objective standard. Fiat money only appears when the state goes a step further and abandons the objective standard, coined money, which the state alone can mint and which may have a value superior to that of the commodity of which it is composed, is at the most a first step in the direction of representative money."[35]

The concept of the intrinsic value of money considered important by gold standard supporters, including Simmel and the Austrians, receives little support from Keynes. In his view, these people with their emphasis on the intrinsic value of money are pursuing a "mirage" or a "will-o'-the-wisp." It is better, he argues, to substitute for the notion of the value of money the notion of the general purchasing power of money. This substitution implies a very different pattern of thought that, in turn, entails a different way of conducting monetary policy. The purchasing power of money is viewed as dependent upon the price level of the goods and services in which money income is expended. The concept implies a certain cause-and-effect relationship. The purchasing power of money is high if prices are low and vice versa. The monetary authorities for their part working under this concept aim at stabilizing the purchasing power of money by influencing the general level of prices for goods and services including wages.

If the monetary authorities, on the other hand, are operating under the concept of the value of money, they have no choice but to stabilize the value of money. Under these circumstances, the value of money is the "cause," and the price level is the "effect." A commodity standard such as the gold standard makes such a task easier. Thus, the value of money (i.e., dollar, pound, franc, dinar, etc.) is defined in terms of the commodity (e.g., gold). The job of the authorities is to keep the currency convertible into, say gold, the commodity at the official price. In effect, instead of concerning itself with the general price level, the authority is concerned with only the price, which is the value of money.

This is the relationship under the gold standard that advocates argue in its support. For a contractual society, argue gold standard advocates, free convertibility into gold is a principal plank upon which such a society rests. Diminish the importance of the value of the money concept and you undermine the base on which a contractual society rests. They argue that Keynes' concept of the general purchasing power lends itself to state manipulation of money and inflation or instability.

In fact, Keynes' detractors argue first—thanks to his *Treatise on Money*—an opposite view of money gained currency whose ultimate consequences since the Bretton Woods agreement has been to sever all links between gold and money in 1971. For all practical purposes, the world is now an irredeemable paper (or fiat) monetary standard.[36]

NOTES

1. See Milton Friedman, *Money Mischief: Episodes in Monetary History* (New York: Harcourt Brace Jovanovich 1992), chapters 1 and 2.

2. For a full discussion of these and related issues, see Milton Friedman and Anna J. Schwartz, *Monetary Statistics of the United States* (New York: Columbia University Press, 1970), Part 1. "Definition of Money," pp. 89–197.

3. Friedman, *Money Mischief*, p. 14.

4. Ibid., p. 15.

5. Ibid. See especially Friedman, *Money Mischief*, Chapter 3, "The Crime of 1873," pp. 51–79.

6. See George Macesich, *Political Economy of Money: Emerging Fiat Monetary Regime* (Westport, Conn.: Greenwood, 1999).

7. Milton Friedman, "Monetary Policy: Theory and Practice," *Journal of Money, Credit and Banking*, February 1982, p. 101.

8. Milton Friedman, *The Counter-Revolution in Monetary Theory*, First Wincott Memorial Lecture (London: Institute of Economic Affairs, 1970).

9. S. Herbert Frankel, *Two Philosophies of Money: The Conflict of Trust and Authority* (New York: St. Martin's Press, 1977) and review of Frankel's study by David Laidler in *Journal of Economic Literature*, June 1979, pp. 570–572; S. Herbert Frankel, *Money and Liberty* (Washington, D.C.: American Enterprise Institute for Public Policy Research, 1980).

10. Georg Simmel, *The Philosophy of Money* (translation by T. Bottomore and D. Frisby, with Introduction by D. Frisby) (London and Boston: Routledge and Kegan Paul, 1978).

11. Simmel,

12. Laidler,

13. David Laidler and Robert Rowe, "Georg Simmel's Philosophy of Money: A Review for Economics," *Journal of Economic Literature*, March 1982: 102.

14. Ibid., p. 103.

15. Frankel, *Two Philosophies of Money*, p. 86.

16. Ibid., p. 4.

17. Ibid., p. 95.

18. Ibid., p. 6.

19. Ibid.; and Milton Friedman, "The Role of Monetary Policy," in *The Optimum Quantity of Money and Other Essays* (Chicago: Aldine Publishing, 1969), p. 99.

20. Frankel, *Two Philosophies of Money,* p. 89.

21. Ibid., p. 92.

22. Ibid., p. 5.

23. Simmel, *The Philosophy of Money,* p. 160. He writes,

The most serious repercussions upon exchange transactions will follow from this situation, particularly at the moment when the government's own resources are paid in devalued money. The numerator of the money fraction—the prices of commodities—rises proportionately to the increased supply of money only after the large quantities of new money have already been spent by the government, which then finds itself confronted again with a redeemed supply of money. The temptation then to make a new issue of money is generally irresistible, and the process begins all over again . . . temptation whenever money is not closely linked with a substance of limited supply. . . . Today we know that only precious metals, and indeed only gold, guarantee the requisite qualities, and in particular limitation of quantity; and that paper money can escape the dangers of misuse by arbitrary inflation only if it is tied to initial value established by law or by the economy.

24. John Maynard Keynes, *Monetary Reform* (London: Harcourt Brace, 1924).

25. John Maynard Keynes, *Economic Consequences of the Peace* (London: Macmillan, 1920).

26. F. A. Hayek, "The Keynes Century: The Austrian Critique," *The Economist*, June 11, 1983: 39.

27. Milton Friedman, "The Keynes Centenary: A Monetarist Reflects," *The Economist*, June 4, 1983: 19.

28. Ibid., p. 19.

29. John Maynard Keynes, *A Treatise in Money*, vol. 1. (London: Macmillian, 1930), p. 3, 4.

30. Keyes writes, "The difference is like that between the King of England (whoever he may be) and King George. A contract to pay ten years hence a weight of gold equal to the weight of the King of England is not the same thing as a contract to pay a weight of gold equal to the weight of the individual who is now King George. It is for the State to declare when the time comes, who the King of England is." Ibid., p. 4.

31. Ibid.

32. Ibid.

33. Ibid., p. 6.

34. Ibid., p. 8.

35. Ibid., p. 9.

36. Macesich, *Political Economy of Money*.

Chapter 2

Supply and Demand for Money

DEMAND FOR MONEY

In the neoclassical analysis, the demand for money is functionally related to income interest rates and some types of wealth. The question of the nature of income in the money demand function has long been under debate: the current income, real income, or Milton Friedman's permanent income. The nature of the interest rate also commands attention: the short-term government bond rate or the money market rate on private debt. In effect, the arguments or variables that enter the demand function for money and the definition of the quantity of money appropriate for the demand function have received substantial attention in both the recent and distant past. A number of studies seem to suggest that in the long run, the demand function for money may not be stable. To judge from some of these studies, the function shifts over different phases of the cycle; no unique and stable function would therefore be obtained.[1]

Money is one of the forms in which individuals can hold their assets. In some economies, a small interest income can be obtained from assets that are also used for money. But the desire to hold cash cannot be explained by this fact; nevertheless, there are many instances of money yielding no interest and being held nevertheless. Two peculiar and interrelated characteristics of money have usually been emphasized in theories that set it apart from other assets. The first is that money is acceptable as a means of exchange for goods and services, and second, its market value is generally highly predictable. These two characteristics are not the exclusive property of money. Other assets also possess them in varying degrees. However, unlike other assets, money is universally accepted as a means of exchange, and its value is usually more predictable than that of other assets.

The three motives introduced by J. M. Keynes are the transactions, the precautionary, and the speculative motives. Keynes said, in developing in detail the motives for liquidity preference, that the subject was substantially the same as that which has been sometimes discussed under the heading of the "Demand for Money."[2]

Keynes postulated that the level of transactions undertaken by an individual and also by the aggregate of individuals would be in a stable relationship to the level of income. Hence, the so-called transactions demand for money would be proportional to the level of income. The use of the term *transactions motive*, however, was confined to describing the necessity of holding cash to bridge the gap between receipt of payments and the disbursement of such proceeds, or to bridge the interval between purchase and realization.

According to Keynes, the precautionary motive concerns the two aspects of the demand for balances: first, the demand for cash as a proportion of assets to provide for contingencies requiring sudden expenditure and for unforeseen opportunities of advantageous purchases; and second, the demand for an asset whose value is fixed in terms of money to meet a subsequent liability, that is, bank indebtedness, fixed in terms of money.[3] Keynes suggested that the demand for money that came from the precautionary motive would depend largely on the level of income.

Earlier writers suggested that uncertainty about the future was one of the factors that might be expected to influence the demand for money. Keynes' analysis of the speculative motive represents an attempt to formalize one aspect of this suggestion and to draw conclusions from it. In effect, the aggregate demand for money to satisfy the speculative motive, according to Keynes, usually shows a continuous response to gradual changes in the rate of interest.[4] Furthermore, he said, "it is important to distinguish between changes in the rate of interest . . . due to changes in the supply of money . . . and those which are primarily due to changes in expectations affecting the liquidity function itself."[5]

Accordingly, the Keynesian theory of liquidity preference separates the demand for money into two parts:

$$M^D = L_1 (Y) + L_2 (r). \qquad (2.1)$$

The first part, $L_1 (Y)$, based on transactions and precautionary motives, is treated as a function of income; the second part, $L_2 (r)$, is based on speculative motives as a function of the interest rate. This analytical breakthrough by Keynes was significant in that it placed the demand for money in a behavioral framework consistent with the concept of utility maximization in an uncertain world, and away from the restrictive notion of institutionally determined payment schedules. Later economists, however, have found that the demand for transaction balances was also interest elastic.[6] Since the alternative to holding cash for transaction purposes is short-run assets (including time deposits), their rate of interest should be treated as an argument in the demand function for money.

Moreover, people's behavior in holding cash balances is affected not only by the transactions, the precautionary, and the speculative motives, as dictated by Keynesian theory, but also by their expectations of changes in the price level.[7] The alternative cost of carrying over one's wealth from one period to the next in the form of cash balances is the profit one could obtain by carrying over this wealth in the form of other assets, such as commodities and bonds.

The symmetry between the rate of interest and the rate of price increase brings out the fact that even the existence of certain anticipations of a price increase will not cause an absolute flight from cash. Instead, just as in the case of the interest rate, it will simply cause individuals to adjust their holding of real cash balances so that the marginal utility the liquidity cash balances provide compensates individuals for the opportunity costs of holding these balances.

Therefore, the expected rate of change of the price level must be interpreted as an expected rate of return on money holding. Other things being equal, the higher the expected rate of return to money holding, the more it will be held; the lower it is the less it will be held. The expected rate of change of the price level becomes a potentially important variable in the demand-for-money function. Since the actual rate of change in prices of the immediate past is probably the basic determinant of present expected change in prices, for simplicity, the former may be substituted as an argument explaining the demand for money. The demand for money may assume the basic form:

$$M/P^D = f\,(r^s,\, Y/P,\, Z).\tag{2.2}$$

Where M^D is nominal money stock, P is the price level, r^s is the short term market rate of interest, Y/P is the real income, and $Z = P - P_{-1}$ is the rate of change in the price level. In equation (2.2) partial derivatives of M^D/P with respect to r^s and Z are expected to be negative, and with respect to Y/P to be positive.

SUPPLY OF MONEY

The pure theory of the demand for money assumes that the nominal supply of money is given and is varied at the discretion of the monetary authorities and government. Demand theory sets out to analyze the effects on general equilibrium of a change in the nominal quantity of money or of a change in demand for money arising from an exogenous change in tastes. Demand theory also explicitly assumes that the monetary authorities and government can control the nominal quantity of money. In contrast to this view, there is a school that sees the money supply responding to demand; it therefore concludes that there is no point in attempting to control the economy by monetary policy. Hence, a theory of money, if it is to be consistent, requires that supply be determined independently of the money demand, and if the theory is to be of use, it must allow that the central bank can control the quantity of money in the hands of the public.[8]

Early theories of money supply developed a mechanistic approach that did not allow for the possibility of ratios being behavioral functions of economic variables. This stage of the theory's development is evocative of early quantity and Keynesian multiplier analysis. There is now considerable evidence showing that the supply of money can be expressed as a function of few variables.[9] Basically, there are two types of functions: First, Brunner and Brunner and Meltzer consider money supply as a function of the monetary base, currency-deposit ratio, and reserve-deposit ratio. They contend that, with the monetary base given, the current rate of interest can have very little impact on the money supply.[10] Second, in contrast, Teigen, Goldfield, Smith, Modigliani, Rasche, and Cooper, and Bhattacharya attach importance to the interest rates. A bank's ability to vary the level of excess and borrowed reserves it wishes to hold provides an important reason for treating the money supply as an endogenous variable. The interest responsiveness of excess and borrowed reserves implies a supply function of money that is similarly responsive. To allow the dependence, Teigen has estimated a relationship in which the money supply is made a function of certain Federal Reserve parameters and of interest rates, while the study by Goldfield is a "slightly high-order approach," in that he derives the money supply from bank behavior, a function of the Teigen-type is implicit in his model.

In essence, two main theories of money-supply determination emerge. One is that a stable relation exists between the money supply and reserve base. Accordingly, when the stock of reserves increases or decreases, the money supply will change in a predictable way. Thus, a central bank can control the money supply by controlling total reserves of the banking and monetary systems.

The second theory argues that in the United States, the volume of member banks borrowing from the Federal Reserve System and the volume of excess reserves of Federal Reserve member banks (or the net of the two is free reserves) influence bank behavior in such a way that the rate of change of bank deposits and money supply can be predicted from these variables. One implication of this money supply theory for the operation of a central bank should be focused on excess reserves and borrowings, or on free reserves, rather than on total reserves in attempting to control the money supply.

The two main theories are not so clearly alternate to each other as they might seem to be at first. Each contains useful insights regarding the behavior of the monetary system. If they are combined, each may contribute an essential element of a more satisfactory explanation of changes in the money supply than can be obtained from either of them separately. This action develops a way to incorporate variation in excess reserves and borrowings, or the two combined in free reserves, in a theory of money supply determination. By so doing, we synthesize the two basic approaches described above.

The derivation of the money supply model proceeds as follows: monetary base (H), or high-powered money as it is frequently referred to, is defined to include all monetary assets capable of being used as banking reserves. It is represented by

$$H = C + R, \qquad (2.3)$$

where R = high-powered money inside the banks (banking reserves), and C = high-powered money outside banks (currently supplied by government). C is defined as

$$C = C_p + C_b, \tag{2.4}$$

where C_p = currency held by the nonbank public, and C_b = currency held by commercial banks.

In the United States, currency held by commercial banks (vault cash) can also be counted as required reserves, and it can be used for excess reserves. In this case, high-powered money is defined as

$$H = C_p + R, \tag{2.5}$$

where total bank reserves (R) are defined as

$$R = R_r + R_e + C_b. \tag{2.6}$$

In either case, the definition of high-powered money is not changed.

Similarly, total bank reserves are defined as

$$R = R_r + R_e, \tag{2.7}$$

where R_r = required reserves of member banks, and R_e = excess reserves of member banks. Money supply is defined as

$$M_1^s = C_p \, DD, \tag{2.8}$$

or

$$M_2^s = C_p \, D, \tag{2.9}$$

where DD refers to demand deposits and D the sum of derived and time deposits.

Regardless of whether definition (2.8) or (2.9) of money supply is used, the arguments remain the same. But the data on R_r will be different for demand deposits and aggregate deposits. Without loss of generality, if we further assume the public desires to hold a fixed proportion g (0 < gl) of money supply in currency, and that the banking system maintains a fixed cash-deposit ratio $n(0 < n < 1)$, then we get

$$C_p = g_1 \, M_1^s, \tag{2.10}$$

or

$$C_p = g_2 \, M_2^s \tag{2.11}$$

and

$$C_b = n_1 \, DD = n_1 \, (M_1^s - c_1) = n_1 \, (1 - g) \, M_1^s, \tag{2.12}$$

or

$$C_b = n_2 \, D = n_2 \, (M_2^s - C_p) = n_2 \, (1 - g) \, M_2^s. \tag{2.13}$$

If K is the required reserve ratio $(0 < K < 1)$ then we can write

$$R_r = K_1 \, DD = K_1 \, (M_1^s - C_p), \tag{2.14}$$

or

$$R_r = K_2 \, D = K_2 \, (M_2^s - C_p). \tag{2.15}$$

Here we note that if K, g, and n are constant, the authorities can control the money supply by fixing the monetary base (H). But if (H) is held constant and K or g, or n changes, then the money supply does not remain constant. The reserve-deposit ratio rises as commercial banks keep larger reserves to ensure solvency in the face of increased uncertainty.

Thus, the money supply at any moment is the result of portfolio decisions by the central bank, the commercial banks, and the public. Whether the central banks, by controlling the monetary base, can actually achieve fairly precise control over the money supply depends on whether the link between the monetary base and bank reserves and the money supply (the monetary base–bank reserves–money supply linkage) is fairly tight and therefore predictable. If there is a tight linkage, the monetary authorities can formulate their policies and achieve any particular target for the money supply; on the other hand, if there is significant unpredictable slippage and the central bank control over the money supply is not sufficiently precise to achieve a given target, it will necessarily have to formulate its policies in terms of other variables it can control. The variable used to confine the central bank's objective, or to implement its policy decisions, must therefore be one it can control within reasonable limits.

Let U be the unborrowed monetary base, defined as

$$U = H - R_b, \tag{2.16}$$

Where R_b refers to the borrowings by commercial banks from the central bank. Then we obtain

$$U_1 = C_p + C_b + R_b + (R_e - R_b) = (g + n - ng + K - Kg) M_1^s + R_f. \tag{2.17}$$

$$U_2 = C_g + n - ng (+ k - kg) M_2^s + R_f, \tag{2.18}$$

where $R_f = R_e - R_b$ is free reserves.

"Free reserves" are used in this discussion rather than the component "excess reserves" and "borrowings" in part for convenience in exposition and in part because there are plausible theoretical grounds for this procedure. The question of whether excess reserves and borrowings should be treated separately or as combined in free reserves will be kept open.

Member banks of the Federal Reserve System in the United States hold excess reserves because they want to be able to meet cash demands of their depositors without drawing down their legal reserves and hence incurring a penalty cost on reserve deficiencies. Excess reserves, however, are assumed to be nonearning assets. The opportunity cost to the banks is the yield they must give up by not acquiring an earning asset such as government securities.

Banks are supposedly discouraged from borrowing from the central bank except to meet unexpected short-term contingencies. Nevertheless, there is some interest elasticity with respect to the discount rate. If the discount rate is substantially below the yield that can be earned on short-term government securities, commercial banks will prefer to borrow from the central bank instead of selling these securities. Thus, the lower the discount rate relative to short-term market interest rates, the lower the level of free reserves will be if the central bank does not take offsetting measures. That is, the level of the discount rate determines to some extent whether banks sell short-term securities or draw down their excess reserves.

Without specifying the direction of causality between the discount rate and the short-term interest rate, the free reserves question can be treated as a function of the discount rate (r^d) and the short-term market rate of interest (r^s). Free reserves will also vary with the lagged reserve ratio of commercial banks V_{-1}, defined as the ratio of the holdings of reserves by banks to their deposit of the beginning of each year. V_{-1} is a lagged endogenous variable, as its components are all determined within the system. These considerations suggest that the free reserves function may assume the basic form

$$R_f = h^* (r^d, r^s, v_{-1}). \tag{2.19}$$

In equation (2.19) partial derivatives of R_f with respect to r^d and v_{-1} are expected to be positive, and those with respect to r^s to be negative. Combining equations (2.3) and (2.4) and solving for M_q^s, $q = 1, 2$, we obtain the basic form of the money supply function.

$$M_q^s = h (U, r^d, r^s, v_{-1}). \tag{2.20}$$

In equation (2.20) partial derivatives of M_q^s with respect to U and r^s are expected to be positive, and those with respect to r^d and v_{-1} to be negative.

If free reserves are assumed to be linear of the basic form

$$R_f = a_0 + a_2 r^d - a_3 r^s + a_s v_{-1}, \tag{2.21}$$

we then obtain the money function

$$M_q^s = 1/m (-a_0 + a_1 U = a_2 r^2 + a_3 r^s - a_4 v_{-1}), \tag{2.22}$$

where $a = 1, 2$ and $m = (y + n - ng + K - Kg)$.

The money supply function postulated in equation (2.22) differs from the money supply function derived by other authors. Some authors have distinguished the actual from the potential money supply, but this is not the case in equation (2.22). It also differs from authors who have introduced the differential between the discount rate and a short-term market interest rate as an explicit variable.

THE GLOBAL DIMENSION

The reemergence of the long dormant view, with roots going back more than two hundred years that money and monetary policy are indeed important in the global economy, is underscored by the work on the monetary approach to the balance-of-payments. As in the quantity theory statement of Milton Friedman, the essential assumption in the monetary approach is that an aggregate demand function for money that is a stable function of a relatively small number of aggregate economic variables does exist. In this sense, it makes the same assumption as in the moderate Keynesian view. Like the classical theory of money, the monetary approach assumes the longer run view, for the most part, of a fully employed economy as the norm rather than the exception.

A country's size is irrelevant to the monetary approach. A small country viewed as facing a parametric set of world prices and interest rates presents no theoretical difficulty in taking demand and supply functions as dependent on prices rather than prices themselves as parameters. Country size is important on the monetary side of the analysis. For instance, a large country such as the United States whose national currency is internationally acceptable may, as a result of following an inflationary domestic monetary policy, force an accumulation of its money in foreign hands and so lead to world inflation rather than a loss in its international reserves. The post–World War II era is a good illustration of such a case.

FRIEDMAN AND SCHWARTZ ON THE MONEY SUPPLY

A useful analytical apparatus for dealing with the supply of money is given in Friedman and Schwartz's *A Monetary History of the United States 1867–1960*.[11] In this study they analyze the proximate determinants of the nominal stock of money. Three determinants are discussed. The first is high-powered money (H), or the kinds of money that can be issued for currency or as reserves, defined as the sum of specie and obligations of monetary authorities. The second is deposit/reserve rates. The third determinant is the proportion of deposits and currency that the public chooses to hold. This proportion, denoted by the ratio D/C, depends on the related usefulness of the two media, on the cost of holding them, and perhaps on income.

Based on this notion, Friedman and Schwartz derive the relationship of the stock of money with the three determinants in the following manner:

$$M = C + D,$$

$$H = C + R,$$

$$M = \frac{C + D}{C + R} = \frac{\frac{D}{R}\left(1 + \frac{D}{C}\right)}{\frac{D}{R} + \frac{D}{C}}$$

or

$$M = H\,\frac{\frac{D}{R}\left(1 + \frac{D}{C}\right)}{\frac{D}{R} + \frac{D}{C}} \qquad (2.23)$$

where C = currency held by the public, D = savings, time, and demand deposits by the public, M = money supply, R = bank reserves, H = high-powered money.

The findings of Friedman and Schwartz in their study for the period 1867–1960 in the United States suggested that, in the long run, changes in the broadly defined money stock were due primarily to changes in high-powered money, but that changes in the other two determinants proportioned a large share of the changes in the cycles, with the currency ratio being more relevant for mild cycles and the deposit ratio more relevant for critical situations.

CAGAN ON THE MONEY SUPPLY

In the spirit of the Friedman and Schwartz study Phillip Cagan focuses on the sources of covariation between money and business activity by examining the factors affecting the amount of money supplied.[12] He places greater emphasis on the behavior of the three sectors of economy that affect the amount of money supplied: the government, the public, and the commercial banks. The behavior of the government sector is reflected in high-powered money. The public holds currency in circulation that is part of high-powered money and affects the distribution of high-powered money between itself and commercial banks by changing the ratio of currency outside commercial banks to the total money stock. Commercial banks affect the money stock by their decisions on the level at which to maintain the ratio of high-powered money reserves to deposits held by the public. Based on the above, Cagan derives the following identities:[13]

$$H = C + R$$

$$\frac{H}{M} = \frac{C}{M} + \frac{R}{D} - \frac{C}{M} \times \frac{R}{D}$$

or

$$M = \frac{H}{\frac{C}{M} + \frac{R}{D} - \frac{C}{M} \times \frac{R}{D}}, \qquad (2.24)$$

where H = high-powered money, C = currency in circulation, D = commercial bank deposits held by the public, M = the money stock, defined as M = C + D, and R = high-powered money reserves. The last equation for (2.24) expresses the total money stock in terms of the quantity of high-powered money, the currency-money ratio, and the reserve-deposit ratio. Cagan referred to these three variables as the determinants of the money stock.

Cagan's findings confirmed Friedman's results on the secular movements, but they did not attribute significance to the deposit ratio, considering the currency ratio as the relevant factor in determining cyclical movements. Cagan went one step further to conclude that the movements in the currency ratio were the results of changes in economic activity.

It is interesting to note that none of the studies conducted by Friedman and Schwartz or Cagan found interest rates as having a large influence in movements of the money stock.

OTHER VIEWS ON THE MONEY SUPPLY

The studies by Friedman and Schwartz and Cagan provide a framework within which ex post changes or rates of change in the supply of money can be allocated to several determinants. Other views attempt to construct simultaneous models of the monetary sector thereby assuming that the crucial variables are mutually determined and so place the supply of money within the context of a model. Other differences arise among the various views that the supply of money places emphasis on one or another determinant.

In general, there appear to be two main views on the determination of the supply of money. One is that in general there is a stable relation between the money supply and the reserve base. Accordingly, a central bank can control the money supply by controlling total reserves of the banking and monetary systems. The other view is that the volume of bank borrowing from the central bank and the volume of excess reserves of banks influence bank behavior in such a way that the rate of change of bank deposits and money supply can be predicted from these variables. Therefore, a central bank should focus its attention on excess reserves and borrowings, or on free reserves, rather than on total reserves in attempting to control the money supply.

PERMANENT INCOME MODELS

Recent developments in the demand for money include Friedman's arguments in favor of including human wealth as an influence on the demand for money. In its general form, wealth, both human and nonhuman, is regarded as the constraint on money demand, and the fundamentals of capital theory are applied to the problem of assets equilibrium.

Friedman's empirical work is aimed at offering a theoretical explanation for the discrepancy between the secular and cyclical behavior of income velocity. He finds that the supply of money generally rises secularly at a considerably higher rate than money income does. Thus, income velocity tends to fall over long periods as income rises. During cycles, on the other hand, the money stock usually increases during expansions at a lower rate then money income and either continues to rise during contractions or falls at a lower rate than money income. Over the cycle, therefore, income velocity rises and falls with income, that is, it moves procyclically. The issue, then, is that in the long run the income elasticity of the demand for money is considerably above unity, whereas in the short run it is less than unity.

In an attempt to explain this cyclical phenomenon and to examine the relationship between the stock of money and money income, Friedman suggests that the demand for money, defined as currency plus demand and time deposits of commercial banks, is a function of permanent income rather than measured income. Permanent income is measured as an exponentially weighted average of prior measured income and is considered to fluctuate less over the cycle than the corresponding measured magnitudes. If permanent income rather than measured income is used to compute cyclical velocity, then the latter would fluctuate countercyclically, and the conflict between secular and cyclical velocity would be resolved. The particular money demand function formulated by Friedman is

$$M/NP_p = a\,(Y_p/NP_p)^b, \tag{2.25}$$

where M is currency plus demand and time deposits at commercial banks, P_p is the permanent price lead, Y_p is permanent nominal aggregate income, N is population, and a and b are parameters. This equation states that permanent real balances per capita are a function of permanent real income per capita. Friedman concludes that money is a luxury with a per capita income elasticity of 1.8. However, the rate of interest is shown to be a negligible affect. In fact, of the many experiments that have been performed, only one, which was carried out by Friedman for the period 1869–1957, failed to find a relationship between the demand for money and the interest rate. Friedman reasoned that, since the greater part of variations in the rate of interest takes place within the business cycle, a demand-for-money function fitted to data that abstract from the cycle, if it is used to predict cyclical fluctuations in the demand for money, should yield errors in prediction related to the rate of interest. He therefore took data on the average values of the variables concerned over each business cycle. The variable used was money defined to include time deposits and permanent income and to them was fitted a log-linear regression whose parameters were then used to predict annual variations in the velocity of circulation. He found no close relationship between the errors of prediction and the rate of interest.

However, we observe closely that if interest rates on time deposits are positively correlated with other interest rates, then demand for time deposits being directly related to their interest rates is also often positively related to other interest rates. This is why the inclusion of time deposits in the definition of money often leads to the rejection of the Keynesian liquidity preference hypothesis in empirical analysis. It may also be the reason why Friedman and many others have found no significant inverse relationship between money demand and interest rate.

OTHER MODELS OF MONEY

Clearly monetary economics is a vast field. Recent discussions in the field focus on three modeling strategies.[14] Two of these strategies, "representative-agent models" and "overlapping-generation models," draw on a common methodological approach in building equilibrium relations explicitly on the foundation of optimizing behavior of individual agents. The third modeling strategy focuses on equilibrium relations that are not derived directly from any decision problem. Critics describe such models as "ad hoc," while their proponents describe them as convenient approximations. The proponents may well be right thanks to their ability in helping economists gain insights into monetary problems.[15]

Other economists find the representative-agent models more useful because they can be more directly compared to actual data. In fact this is one reason that real-business-cycle models employ the representative-agent approach. These models also emphasize the medium-of-exchange role that money plays. Still other economists use a variety of ad hoc models that find helpful in highlighting key issues in affecting the linkages between monetary and real economic phenomena.[16]

NOTES

1.   Scott E. Hein, "Dynamic Forecasting and the Demand for Money," *Federal Reserve Bank of St. Louis Review*, June/July 1980: 13–23, rejects the notion of a constantly shifting money demand relationship and concludes that money is a useful policy instrument. Innovation has had the effect on the demand for money during the turbulent 1970s.

2.   J. M. Keynes, *The General Theory of Employment, Interest, and Money* (New York: Harcourt Brace, 1936), p. 194.

3.   Ibid., pp. 170–71, 195–97.

4.   Ibid., p. 197.

5.   Ibid., p. 197.

6.   In his later writings, Keynes did permit the rates of interest to affect L_1 () as well as L_2 (); see his "Theory of the Rate of Interest" (1937), reprinted in *Readings in the Theory of Income Distribution*, W. Feller and B. F. Healey, eds. (Philadelphia: Blaxiston, 1949), p. 422.

7.   See, for instance, Milton Friedman, "The Demand for Money—Some Theoretical and Empirical Results," *Journal of Political Economy* 67, June 1959: 327–351; D. Laidler, *The Demand for Money: Theories and Evidence* (Scranton, Penn.: International Textbook, 1969), pp. 106–97; Lawrence B. Smith and John W. L. Winder, "Price and Interest Rate Expectations and the Demand for Money in Canada," *Journal of Finance*, June 1979: 671–682; Milton Friedman, "The

Quantity Theory of Money: A Restatement," Milton Friedman, ed., *Studies in the Quantity Theory of Money* (Chicago: University of Chicago Press, 1956).

8.   Harry G. Johnson, *Macroeconomics and Monetary Theory* (London: Gray-Mills, 1971), p. 135.

9.   For a survey of this evidence, refer to A. J. Meigs, *Free Reserves and the Money Supply* (Chicago: University of Chicago Press, 1962); P. H. Hendershoot and F. DeLeeuw, "Free Reserves, Interest Rates and Deposits: A Synthesis," *Journal of Finance* 25, June 1970: 599–614; George Macesich and H. Tsai, *Money in Economic Systems* (New York: Praeger, 1982).

10.   See Meigs, *Free Reserves*; p. 1.

11.   Milton Friedman and Anna J. Schwartz, *A Monetary History of the United States, 1867–1960* (Princeton University Press, 1963); see also, Milton Friedman and Anna J. Schwartz, *Monetary Statistics of the United States* (New York: Columbia University Press, 1970).

12.   Phillip Cagan, *Determinants and Effects of Changes in the Money Stock 1875–1960* (New York: Columbia University Press, 1965).

13.   Ibid.

14.   For a useful summary see Carl E. Walsh, *Monetary Theory and Policy* (Cambridge, Mass.: Massachusetts Institute of Technology, 1998); J. H. Kareken and N. Wallace, eds. *Models of Monetary Economics* (Minneapolis: Federal Reserve Bank of Minneapolis, 1980).

15.   See, for instance, T. J. Sargent, *Dynamic Macroeconomic Theory* (Cambridge, Mass.: Harvard University Press, 1987); B. Champ and S. Freemen, *Modeling Monetary Economies* (New York: J. Wiley, 1994).

16.   See Walsh, *Monetary Theory and Policy*, p. 3.

Chapter 3

Central Banking: The Early Years

THE FIRST AND SECOND UNITED STATES BANKS

A key actor in the formulation and execution of monetary policy are central banks. They are now, for all practical purposes, an arm of the government. Although government-sponsored banks are recorded at the end of the seventeenth century in Europe (Swedish Riksbank, 1668 and Bank of England, 1694) and in the United States in the eighteenth century (First Bank of the United States, 1791–1811 and the Second Bank of the United States, 1816–1836), the original intent was not that they undertake modern central bank functions such as the formulation and execution of monetary policy. These functions evolved over time.

A fundamental issue is the control of these institutions. Experiences in the United States suggest the nature of the problem. The First and Second Banks of the United States are examples of this early experience. These two banks were not central banks in the modern sense. They did, however, perform some central banking functions, such as indirectly regulating state bank note issues and acting as banker for the government, including keeping government deposits.

Since commercial banks in the United States were privately owned and controlled, it was considered appropriate that the First and Second United States Banks should also be controlled in the same way. Naturally, not everyone agreed. For one thing, many in the U.S. Congress did not consider it appropriate that so much financial power be concentrated in private hands for fear of the political and economic abuse such concentration could produce. At the same time, there were also fears that government control could very well subject these banks to political pressure with all its undesirable consequences. Again, American experience underscores the problem.

Resentment and envy were created by both Banks of the United States in their role as depository of the Treasury and their self-assumed role of currency regulator. They kept pressure on the state banks' reserves, thus limiting the ability of state banks credit extension and expansion of their deposit and note liabilities. These feelings were reinforced by states' rights, fear of increasing federal power, and growing monopoly in the country's monetary arrangement. The stage was set for the struggle for monetary supremacy, which has characterized a good deal of American monetary and financial history. One effect of this struggle was to generate considerable public uncertainty over money and the country's monetary system.[1]

Thus, the First Bank's charter was allowed to expire in 1811, and its offices became state banks. In 1814 a general suspension of specie payments occurred, and for the next five years American circulating bank notes (in terms of specie) left much to be desired. The U.S. Treasury found it difficult to operate due to the varying rates of discount in the bank notes of state banks. These difficulties prompted another attempt at national banking. In 1816 the Second Bank of the United States was chartered for twenty years. Once again the Bank collided with local banks and states' rights politicians.

The Suffolk Bank in Boston, which some scholars recognized as a regulator of currency, is an illustration. Unlike the Bank of the United States, which performed its regulatory function as the creditor of local banks, the Suffolk Bank, like the Federal Reserve Banks, performed its regulatory role as their debtor. Nor did the Suffolk Bank have its constitutionality challenged as did the Bank of the United States in 1819 in the now-celebrated Supreme Court decision in *McCulloch v. Maryland*. The Bank's constitutionality ensured, which its detractors denied, freed from prohibitory taxation by states in which it had offices, the Second Bank of the United States enjoyed a brief period of prosperity—a period during which it managed to improve the country's currency circulation while at the same time alienating important sections of government on whose goodwill its survival depended. This is an early illustration of the illusory nature of central bank independence.

President Andrew Jackson's administration, which began in 1829, ushered in a new phase in the continuing and growing struggle for monetary supremacy. Matters were complicated by the fact that the Second Bank of the United States was located in Philadelphia, whose dominant economic role was overtaken by New York. Moreover, New York was the source of the bulk of federal customs receipts. These receipts went to Philadelphia for deposit with the Second Bank, providing considerable irritation to New York merchants and underscoring again the issues of states' rights. The issue was soon brought to national attention when Martin Van Buren, an influential New Yorker, became adviser to President Jackson. Since the Bank's charter was to expire in 1836, the New Yorkers set about getting the deposit of federal funds moved to New York City. This was not difficult to do in view of the political temper of the times. To be sure, the Bank's opponents on Wall Street kept their own counsel; the agrarian and states' rights interests and President Jackson were cultivated to their side. They won. In 1832 President Jackson vetoed the new charter passed by Congress. A few months later Jackson was reelected with a sizable majority. Anticipating the Bank's demise in 1836, Jackson began transferring government deposits to selected banks.

Thereafter came the Specie Circular of 1836 and the Deposit Act, which called for distribution of the federal surplus among several states. The distribution was to be made in 1837 in four installments. Only the first installment was paid in full, and within a year of the Van Buren administration, the Treasury had a deficit of more than $5 million. The New Yorkers, however, did not get their "Big Bank." Instead, the opponents of banking rushed through the Independent Treasury System in 1846. Under this system the banks were denied all federal deposits, the Treasury was required to hold all its funds in its own vaults in gold and silver, and all payments to and by the Treasury were required to be made in coin only.

Contemporaries and more recent students hold the view that the Second Bank of the United States represented an early central bank that had three distinctive methods with which to exercise its discretionary authority and thus affect "favorably" the money supply: it was the depository of federal funds; it possessed numerous branches and it exercised "proper restraint" in its dealings as a private bank.[2]

By skillfully employing these methods, it is held, the Bank was able to wield control over and through the state banks on the money supply. The process of control was simplicity itself: the Bank merely presented the bank notes of the state banks for payments when they fell into its hands. Contemporaries emphasized that the stability of the country's currency depended almost exclusively on this measure. As to the effects of these operations, evidence is presented that state bank notes prior to 1834 had been either driven out of circulation or made redeemable in specie.

It should be pointed out, however, that if the Second Bank could affect the money supply and the economy by "skillfully" employing the methods at its disposal, it could just as well affect the money supply and the economy by "unskillfully" employing the same methods. It does little for the defense of discretionary controls to argue that such controls will always, or even often, be employed "skillfully." And indeed there is little comfort to be found in the ability of "skillful" employment of discretionary controls even by so august a figure as Nicholas Biddle, head of the Second Bank.

Furthermore, even the methods available to the Second Bank for controlling the money supply are subject to several criticisms. In the first instance, the possession of numerous branches might simply have resulted in the circulation of the notes of the Second Bank instead of the notes of state banks. This does not mean that the availability of a relatively uniform currency might not have been economically advantageous. It does mean, however, that the possession of numerous branches is consistent with little or no effect on the total money supply. In the second instance, the exercise of "proper restraint" in its dealings as a private bank is asserted as a method for keeping state banks in debt to the Second Bank. By keeping state banks in debt, it is said, the Second Bank restricted their operations with a threat of a call for specie. The serious employment of this method, however, would almost certainly have resulted in making the Second Bank a smaller institution. Indeed, if it made no loans and issued no notes it could simply go out of business. The real method of control over state banks seems to have stemmed from the Bank's position as a depository for federal funds.[3] In its position as a federal depository, a state bank in all payments to the government had to satisfy the Bank of the United States that its notes were equivalent to specie before the government would receive them, and if the government refused them, a source of extensive circulation was closed. In this matter, the Bank could face a state bank with the alternative of operating on a specie paying basis or having its business severely restricted and the credit of its notes destroyed.

However, in order to see what the real effects of the Bank's actions were on the money supply, one must see what its effect was on international economic movements. The reason for this becomes obvious when one recalls that the United States was on the international specie standard with fixed exchange rates. Under these circumstances a country's first monetary duty is to obey the well-known rules for the operation of that standard. There is little room indeed for a central bank—albeit a primitive one such as the Second Bank—to exercise discretionary authority and to pursue an independent course of action.

Under a specie standard the exchange rates are fixed within specie points, with the result that the internal price level and income in the United States are at first determined by the external events. Thus, the internal price level must be of a value relative to the external price level, such that payments, including capital flows, balance. Consequently, the internal money supply is determined by external conditions, but its composition may be affected by internal monetary circumstances. A special explanation for domestic disturbances can arise only if internal prices move differently from external prices.

Domestic conditions can affect the internal price level and incomes appreciably only insofar as they affect the conditions of external balance. For example, suppose internal monetary (bank credit) expansion threatens suspension of specie payments. A price level sufficiently low relative to the external price level must occur so that a surplus will arise that finances the capital outflow.

If the country is not on a specie standard and fixed exchange rates, the situation is different. Internal monetary changes affect income, the price levels, and exchange rates. Income and the internal price level are no longer rigidly linked to external events. The primacy of external events on internal income and price levels is important because much of the monetary upheaval in the United States during the nineteenth century may have been simply manifestations of disturbances more fundamental in nature. Erratic capital flows into and out of the United States, which characterized important periods of the nineteenth century, are but cases in point. The increase in capital inflows required an increase in the internal stock of money in the United States. The only question was how. An expansion of bank note issues and deposit credit could not be a reason for an increase in the money supply; it would be only one form of a rise that would have occurred in one way or another. Of course the opposite would occur for periods of world deflation and cessation of capital imports.

Consider, for instance, the sharp decline in economic activity in the United States from 1839 to 1843.[4] External prices also declined, and the required internal price fall in the United States was further intensified by the cessation of capital inflow of earlier years and by repatriation of foreign investment. This contraction had important effects on the banking structure in the United States, namely, the destruction of the Second Bank in 1841 (then under a Pennsylvania charter), a 25 percent decrease in the number of banks from 1840 to 1843, and about a 30 percent decrease in the stock of money. The collapse of the banking system was one of the forms by which an adjustment, forced by other circumstances, worked itself out. The price decline abroad, cessation of the large capital inflow of earlier years, repudiation of obligations, suspension of specie payments by some banks, and distrust both at home and abroad in the maintenance of the specie standard by the United States made a sizable decline in prices the only alternative to the abandonment of the specie standard and depreciation of the dollar relative to other currencies. Given the maintenance of the specie standard, such an adjustment was unavoidable; if it had not occurred partly through the banking collapse, it would have done so in some other way, for example, by the export of specie. Along with the rest of the country, the less developed areas, such as in the southern states of Alabama, Mississippi, Florida, Arkansas, Louisiana, Georgia, and the Carolinas, contributed their share to readjustment by banking collapses and repudiation of both domestic and international debt.

Reaction to these various necessary adjustments took many forms, including those already discussed. On the national level, President Andrew Jackson's "hard currency" schemes and the Specie Circular of 1836 are perhaps the best illustrations of reaction against adjustments generated by external factors that required an expansion of the money stock in the United States.[5] On the local level, prohibition against banking in some states is characteristic of the extreme form reaction took to the necessary contraction in the money stock, which was partly manifested in the banking collapse of the later 1830s and early 1840s. Singularly harsh, these attempts are but examples of efforts to tighten the country's monetary straitjacket and to force its monetary radicals to dance to the tune of the specie standard.

The account of confusion and mischief spread by some historians and others who fail to grasp the realities of the specie standard game is best illustrated in the commotion over the Second Bank of the United States. Arthur M. Schlesinger, Jr., for example, argues that the Second Bank was a menace to representative government, and its alleged destruction at the hands of Andrew Jackson fully justified.[6] This eliminated, presumably, the concentration of power over loans and currency circulation from the hands of a relatively small group of men. Thus, Schlesinger would have us believe a dangerous obstacle to American economic expansion was removed. Bray Hammond, on the other hand, defends the Bank in a harsh and serious indictment of the Jacksonians.[7]

Much of the confusion, as noted, arises out of the methods ostensibly available to the Second Bank for controlling the money supply. Some of the contemporary reviews attributed the direct "cause" of the rise in prices in 1834–1836 and subsequent difficulties to the operations of "speculators." Friends of the federal administration and supporters of the Second Bank freely exchanged acrimonious charges, each blaming the other for the country's economic plight. Others simply blamed all three, the speculators as well as the two contestants for monetary supremacy. All groups agreed that something was "wrong" with the money system of the country, but of course disagreed what that "something" was. For example, the federal government emphasized "monopoly" in banking and sought to eliminate such "monopoly" by the removal of government deposits from the Second Bank of the United States and by the elimination of the Bank as a national institution. In addition, the government sought to institute a "hard currency" in the place of existing "bank rags"—bank notes. The supporters of the Second Bank, on the other hand, argued that the new method of handling government deposits was the cause of the surplus that accumulated in the Treasury in 1836. The distribution of the surplus in 1837, they argued, precipitated the crisis of that year and the difficulties that followed. As a solution to the country's economic plight, they called for a recharter of the Second Bank, or similar institution, the return of government deposits, and a "well regulated" bank currency. The term *well-regulated* was usually interpreted to mean according to the "needs of trade."

For almost a decade the struggle for monetary supremacy continued. So too did the uncertainty about the ultimate outcome. In respect to the struggle for monetary supremacy it is worth emphasizing the contrast between the arithmetic and the economics of the situation. The rapid rise in the internal stock of money, prices, and physical volume of trade in the period 1834 to 1836 was coincident with the general external expansion. Coupled with the external expansion was the substantial inflow into the United States of both short-term and long-term capital. Although the capital inflow varied, owing partly to the uncertainty created by the struggle for monetary supremacy, it did not ease completely with the difficulties of 1837 but continued into 1839.[8] Under these external conditions, internal adjustments were required on the part of the United States. The only question was how. If, for example, banks expand or contract their deposits and notes in circulation, this is not, under the assumed conditions, the reason the money supply rises or falls—it is only the form that is taken by a rise or fall that would have occurred one way or another. This is the difference between the arithmetic and economics of a situation. Thus, the withdrawal of government deposits from the Second Bank and the use of state banks as depositories for government funds may well have increased money prices and the surplus in the Treasury, but only because external circumstances in this period required an internal expansion. As was indicated, this does not mean that internal disturbances cannot affect the money supply and prices; they can, but only insofar as they affect the conditions of external balance. It could be, for example, that the internal monetary expansion, coupled with the distribution of the surplus, threatened suspension. This, in turn, would have promoted a capital outflow that would be deflationary.

During the period of suspension, 1837–1838, the situation in the United States was different. Internal monetary changes affected the interest price level, and through it the exchange rate, so the price level was no longer rigidly linked to external price levels. Although to a first approximation the changes in the internal stock of money were determined by the requirements of external balance, the particular way in which changes in the money stock were achieved reflected domestic monetary influences.

We may summarize the pre-1860 American monetary experience with a method devised by Phillip Cagan for analyzing changes in the money stock.[9] Cagan views the stock of money as having three proximate determinants within an identity relationship. The proximate determinants of the money supply are high-powered money (specie), the currency-money ratio (specie-money), and the reserve ratio specie to bank notes and bank deposits in public hands. The reserve ratio referred to is not a legal requirement set by monetary authorities, but the existing ratio of reserves to deposits. Since all high-powered money must be either currency in public hands or reserves held by banks, these variables account completely for changes in high-powered money, with shifts in the composition of cash balances between currency and deposits, and with changes in bank-created deposit and notes outstanding.

Cagan formulates these relationships with an identity.

$$M = \frac{H}{C/M + R/D - (C/M)(R/D)} \qquad (3.1)$$

The variation in M due to changes in the determinants may then be calculated by the formula

$$\frac{d}{dt} \ln M = \frac{d}{dt} \ln H + \frac{M}{H}(1 - R/D)\frac{d}{dt}(-C/M) + \frac{M}{H}(1 - C/M)\frac{d}{dt}(1/RD). \qquad (3.2)$$

Multiplying each component of the right-hand side by $\dfrac{100}{\frac{d}{dt}\ln M}$ yields the effect expressed as a percentage.

The results of the investigation indicate that over the period 1834–1860, the most notable roles were played by changes in the reserve ratio and changes in specie-money ratio; third changes in high-powered money.

Let the variable that contributes the largest short-term effect of the three in any given year be called the "most significant variable" for that year. The evidence indicates that this most significant variable was not the same throughout the twenty-six-year period under review. The results lend some support to the existence of banking and monetary problems even though the disturbances themselves were basically of external origin and the ones to which the banks were reacting.

Such concerns ostensibly prompted the passage of the National Bank Act of 1863 and significant government intervention into the economy. To be sure, the financing of the Civil War by the federal government may well have had a greater weight attached to it than requirements of banking reforms or providing a uniform currency for the country. In conclusion, it is interesting to note that contrary to the views of contemporaries and those of more recent students, the monetary damage done by the initial struggle for monetary supremacy and the uncertainty generated by the struggle, in effect, made a large specie stock desirable rather than producing too rapid a rise in the money supply, which kept the money supply from rising as much as it otherwise would have. All of this, however, was played out against a background of fluctuating capital imports and a specie standard with fixed exchange rates.

Accordingly and to a first approximation, it seems reasonable to conclude that the internal struggle for monetary supremacy was a surface manifestation of a deeper disturbance—the general worldwide expansion and subsequent contraction coupled with a substantial inflow and outflow of capital. The consequent adjustment to the external disturbance at first permitted the internal struggle to continue. For example, the capital inflow enabled the Second Bank to stand against the partisans of "hard currency." At the same time, the inflow of specie enabled the partisans of "hard currency" to press for the elimination of the Bank. However, the internal struggle set in motion forces that in themselves were important.

American experience tends to leave most people skeptical about extension of the "free market" to monetary arrangements—even if workable. As the experience underscores, monetary affairs are seldom left alone. Indeed, they readily become critical political issues of a very explosive nature. Proper institutional constraints are necessary. The international specie standard and fixed exchange rates seemed to keep the American experience within prescribed bounds. Even so, it did not always work well.

THE BANK OF ENGLAND

It is to the Bank of England and its founding in 1694 that we turn as the usual dating for beginnings of central banking. The Bank's origins as an institution began with financial promoters of the time and a nearly bankrupt English government.

England's civil wars ended in 1688 with the removal of King James II and the installation of William and Mary to the throne. With the Whig party now in favor and the Tory party out of power, monopoly privileges flowed to the Whigs. This served to reinforce their policy of mercantilism and imperial expansion for the greater glory of the Crown and their own profit. All of this required money and credit. After more than a half century of civil wars, prospects for the government to obtain both were not favorable due to its poor credit rating including a poor record of repayment. Savings were not forthcoming from the public, and taxation was not politically feasible.

The problem was put before a committee of the House of Commons in 1693. A solution came in a proposal from a private group to form the Bank of England, which would issue notes to fill the savings gap and so finance the country's debt. The private group agreed to buy government bonds if the group could do so with the newly created notes. In effect the appearance was created that the government's debt was being properly financed by a legitimate bank.

As soon as the Bank of England was chartered by Parliament in 1694 there was a rush by various members and King William himself to become shareholders in the new money creating institution.[10] In order to enhance its credibility and prestige, the Bank of England, aided and abetted by the government, was clothed with an air of mystery which still continues more than three centuries later.

Although the English government was initially urged to grant the Bank notes legal tender power, the government refused. Instead, the government gave the new Bank the advantage of holding all government deposits as well as the power to issue new notes to pay for the government. The idea of placing government deposits in the Bank was adopted later, as noted earlier, by both the First and Second Banks of the United States. Unlike the experiences of both United States Banks, however, the relations between the Bank of England and the government were such that it could expect the government to come to its assistance whenever necessary, and indeed, full government support to the Bank was always forthcoming.

To be sure, the Bank's creation resulted from the government's need for money and its promoter's desire for profits. In this the Bank set a pattern for the formation of central banks in other countries. Indeed, by the middle of the eighteenth century the Bank had attained a leading position in the country's financial structure. In the closing years of the eighteenth century the Bank's holdings of public securities averaged more than 75 percent of its total portfolio. In addition to arranging for short-term government financial needs, the Bank also had responsibility for the long-term, or funded, government debt, of which it owned a considerable fraction. Its private business was chiefly of two types. It accepted deposits from and maintained drawing accounts for wealthy individuals and business firms, and it discounted bills of exchange and promissory notes for London merchants.

Equally important was the fact that the Bank was the holder of the country's gold reserve. This function was unofficial and largely unacknowledged. By the close of the eighteenth century the Bank had already begun to assume some of the characteristics of a "central bank."

The fact is that the English banking system from 1750 to 1844 was far from ideal in its contribution to either stability or growth of the economy as a whole.[11] The monopoly of the Bank of England, the gross inefficiency of the Mint, the restrictions on small notes, the Resumption Act of 1819, the piecemeal and half-hearted reforms of 1826 and 1833, and finally the Peel's Act of 1844 did little to help the English economy. The country's financial and banking system, though second rate, did respond to the needs and demands of the times.[12]

Important reforms were implemented in England with Peel's Act of 1844, which provided that further increases in rates by the Bank of England must be backed 100 percent by acquisitions of gold and silver; no new bank of issue could be established; the average note issue of each existing country bank could be no greater than the existing amount of issue; banks would lose their note issue rights if they were merged into or bought by another bank, these rights being largely transferred to the Bank of England.

The reformers, however, overlooked the fact that a monopoly bank privileged by the government could lead to abuse in practice. Monopoly power granted by government would be used and likely abused. Moreover, the reformers failed to take into account that demand deposits are as fully a part of the money supply as bank notes. Deprived of the right of note issue, banks (including the Bank of England) began to issue deposits. The country banks relied on the Bank of England to issue notes, which remained legal tender, and turned to the creation of deposits.

The resulting inflationary booms and busts of bank credit after 1844 underscored the shortcomings of the reforms. As the crises arose, foreign and domestic citizens called upon banks for redemption of their notes. The Bank of England was able to get the government to suspend Peel's Act—requiring 100 percent issue of new Bank of England notes allowing the Bank to issue enough fractional reserve legal tender notes—to bail out the entire banking system. The Act was periodically suspended (1847, 1857, 1866, 1914) and finally scrapped in 1928, whereupon any further note issues could be simply authorized by government without an act of Parliament.

The important monetary and banking controversies that dominated the first half of the nineteenth century continue into the closing years of the twentieth century, including whether a central bank is necessary.[13] Indeed, the foundations of the theory of central banking under commodity and paper standards received considerable attention as did banking and fixed and flexible exchange rates in an open economy.

OTHER EARLY BANKS

The Bank of Amsterdam was founded in 1609 in response to a petition of cloth importers.[14] It was a public bank, a deposit bank, and an exchange bank; it was not a credit bank. Adam Smith's discussion is well known concerning Amsterdam and the need to develop bank money in which bills of exchange can be paid. The first state deposit bank was the Bank of St. George in Genoa, which was established in 1407. The same century also saw the development of deposit banks in Spain and Sicily. Their purpose was to provide the public with a valid money in place of uncertain coins then in circulation.

The forerunners of these early public banks go back much further in time. Thus, early bankers undertook to clear mercantile payments in addition to their commerce, shipping, and money changing as early as the fourteenth century. Even earlier in the thirteenth century Venice had arrangements for transferring money.

Kindleberger underscores the primitive nature of these early banks of deposit.[15] To effect transfers on their books in person, the payer and the payee were required to appear together at the bank. This was later broadened to include meeting with a notary. Owing to the state's requirement that they pay out only good coin, they were unwilling to accept questionable coins at face value. Eventually they made arrangements with the state Mints, where coins of questionable value were melted and restruck. Other functions were also eventually acquired, such as holding funds in escrow to await disposition in legal proceedings.

These early banks, at least in theory, were not discount or lending banks. They did not create money but served a system of 100 percent reserves. Overdrafts were forbidden, but difficult to observe in practice particularly in face of a public emergency. Owing to the chaos in the coinage and the convenience of a deposit at the bank (safety of the money and a strong likelihood that one received money of quality), bank money went to a premium over other currency. For the most part bank money ran about 5 percent over currency. If it went higher, the bank would usually buy coin with bank money; if lower it would sell. Indeed, some of the bank's profits were earned from such arbitrage.[16]

The Bank of Amsterdam (1609) served as a precedent for the Riksbank (Bank of Sweden), which was organized in 1656 and divided from the beginning into two departments: an exchange bank patterned after the Bank of Amsterdam and a lending bank.[17] The Riksbank was taken over by the state in 1668, which makes it the oldest central bank in the world. Before its takeover it issued the first bank notes in Europe (1661). As a substitute for coin, bank notes ranked third in usage following bills of exchange and deposits.

NOTES

1. See George Macesich, *The Politics of Monetarism: Its Historical and Institutional Development* (Totowa, N.J.: Rowman and Allanheld, 1984).

2.   See, for example, R.C.H. Catterall, *The Second Bank of the United States* (Chicago: University of Chicago Press, 1903); D. R. Dewey, *The Second United States Bank* (Washington, D.C.: Government Printing Office, 1910); W. B. Smith, *Economic Aspects of the Second Bank of the United States* (Cambridge: Harvard University Press, 1953); and Brag Hammond, *Banks and Politics in America* (Princeton: Princeton University Press, 1957). The Second Bank of the United States operated from 1836 to 1841 with a State of Pennsylvania charter.

3.   Total government deposits amounted to more than $410 million during the entire period that the Second Bank held them. Average monthly government deposits are estimated by the U.S. Treasury for the period 1819 to 1833 to be $6,717,253. See Macesich, *Politics of Monetarism.*

4.   For a more detailed analysis see George Macesich, "The Source of Monetary Disturbances in the United States, 1834–1845," *Journal of Economic History*, September 1960: 407–434. See also Clark Warburton, "Variations in Economic Growth and Banking Developments in the United States from 1835–1885," *Journal of Economic History*, September 1958: 283–297; T. D. Willett, "International Specie Flows and American Monetary Stability," *Journal of Economic History*, March 1968: 28–50.

5.   Harry N. Scheiber, "The Pet Banks in Jacksonian Politics and Finance, 1833–1841," *Journal of Economic History*, June 1963: 196–214.

6.   Arthur M. Schlesinger, Jr., *Age of Jackson* (Boston: Little, Brown and Company, 1945), pp. 115–131.

7.   See Bray Hammond, *Banks and Politics in America.*

8.   L. H. Jenks, *The Migrations of British Capital to 1875* (New York: A. A. Knopf, 1927), chaps. 3–4.

9.   Phillip Cagan, *Determinants and Effects of Averages in the Money Stock, 1875–1960* (New York: National Bureau of Economic Research, 1965).

10.   See Murray Rothbard, *The Mystery of Banking* (New York: Richardson and Snyder, 1983), pp. 179–190; John Clapham, *The Bank of England* (Cambridge: Cambridge University Press, 1958).

11.   See Rondo Cameron (with the collaboration of Olga Crisp, Hugh T. Patrick, and Richard Tilly), *Banking in the Early Stages of Industrialization: A Study in Comparative Economic History* (New York: Oxford University Press, 1967).

12.   Ibid., p. 59.

13.   See Anna J. Schwartz, "Banking School, Currency School, Free Banking School." John Eatwell, Murray Milgate, Peter Newman, eds., in *Money* (New York: W. W. Norton, Co., 1989), pp. 41–49; David Laidler, "The Bullionist Controversy," John Eatwell, Murray Milgate, Peter Newman, eds. in *Money* (New York: W. W. Norton Co., 1989), pp. 60–70; see also Jacob Viner, *Studies in the Theory of International Trade* (New York: Harper and Brothers, 1937), pp. 119–349.

14.   See Charles P. Kindleberger, *A Financial History of Western Europe*, 2nd ed. (New York: Oxford University Press, 1993), p. 50. For early monetary and banking affairs see also Frank C. Spooner *The International Economy and Mone-*

tary Movements in France 1493–1725 (Cambridge: Harvard University Press, 1972) and *Risk at Sea: Amsterdam Insurance and Maritime Europe 1766–1780* (Cambridge: Cambridge University Press, 1981).

15. Kindleberger, *A Financial History of Western Europe*, pp. 49–52.

16. Ibid., p. 51.

17. Ibid., p. 52.

Chapter 4

Central Banking: The Later Years

AN OVERVIEW

The development of central banks from private ownership and involvement in profit-maximizing commercial banking to that of the ultimate source of liquidity and support for individual commercial banks was indeed difficult. No less difficult was the development of the central bank's role in the conduct of monetary policy. In this role the objective was to maintain the internal and external value and integrity of the country's currency. In difficult times such as wars and other crises the central bank served to mobilize the necessary finance to meet the country's needs. In normal times the central bank's focus for much of the nineteenth and early twentieth centuries was to preserve the gold standard and its requirements.

The collapse of the interwar gold standard monetary regime cast in doubt the central banks and monetary policy. Aggregate demand was viewed as better managed by fiscal policy supplemented by direct controls of one kind or another to constrain inflationary pressures and the international sector.

The subsequent erosion of direct controls in the post–World War II years along with the establishment of the Bretton Woods regime of pegged but adjustable exchange rates once again brought central banks on the scene. They assumed their old role of maintaining the value of their national currencies by attempting to hold their pegged value to the U.S. dollar and thereafter and to gold until 1971 when President R. Nixon closed the gold window. These were years when the U.S. dollar was dominant in world financial affairs and the country's central bank—the Federal Reserve System—had the important responsibility of preserving the internal stability of the U.S. dollar. At first successful, internal and external circumstances overwhelmed American monetary policy and the Bretton Woods monetary regime. The requirements of the Vietnam War, the domestic war on poverty, and finally the OPEC oil shock of 1973 served in good measure to bring an end to post-war monetary arrangements including pegged but adjustable exchange rates.

During these years the economic policy focus of the industrialized and developed world was on employment and growth usually along Keynesian lines while preserving the exchange rate peg. When the peg was removed in the early 1970s, countries placed various emphases on policies supporting maximum employment within certain monetary constraints.

At the same time, the goals, instruments, and policy issues of central banks underwent considerable change. Some changes reflect a substantially different domestic and international environment, others are characteristic of individual countries. The timing of changes has varied in many countries depending as they do on considerably different environments in which superficially similar central bank arrangements operate. Thus it is, for instance, that the Bank of France and many other older central banks became increasingly concerned with capital formation thanks in part to the destruction of World War II. Still other central banks were nationalized as were important segments of the economy in Europe and Japan. The Bank of Canada was established in 1934 as a government bank, and, as noted earlier, the oldest of the central banks, the Swedish Riksbank, was a government bank from its creation in the seventeenth century.

For all the changes that have taken place central banks continue to be an important area of government. There have been few radical changes in their position with respect to government and their role in the formulation and implementation of monetary policy as a means for influencing domestic and foreign economic affairs.

REGIONAL AND NATIONAL ASPECTS
OF THE U.S. FEDERAL RESERVE ACT OF 1913

The establishment of twelve Federal Reserve districts in the United States is the consequence of both political and economic forces.[1] These forces are deeply embedded in America's financial history and go back at least to the rise and fall of the first two United States Banks (1791–1811 and 1816–1836). The heat generated by the controversies over the activities of these two institutions and their branches was sufficiently great to be felt even in the twentieth-century attempts at national banking reform.

Attempts to clear the American banking and monetary muddle at the turn of the twentieth century led to the creation by the Aldrich-Vreeland Act of 1908 of the National Monetary Commission. Extensive studies of banking practices before 1910 were made by the monetary commission's staff, but the commission did not limit itself only to studies. It also prepared and recommended a banking reform measure known as the Aldrich Bill. The bill called for the formation of a National Reserve association to be capitalized at $100 million. The Association was to have its central office in Washington and fifteen branches throughout the country, and it was to be owned by the member banks. For all practical purposes it was a central bank with power to rediscount paper for its members, hold deposited reserves without interest, and deal in the open market in U.S. bonds. Moreover, it could also issue asset currency, provided a 50 percent cash reserve was maintained.

Unfortunately for its supporters, the Aldrich Bill rekindled old passions to the extent that it became a political issue during the presidential campaign of 1912. The Democratic party stood opposed to the establishment of a central bank as outlined in the Aldrich Bill. Its political platform of that year called instead for a systematic revision of banking laws and protection from the "Money Trust" composed largely of eastern financial interests. These charges are reminiscent of those leveled at the first two Banks of the United States, which contributed to their downfall.

The Democratic party's victory in the presidential campaign meant the end of the Aldrich Bill. In its place Congress passed the Federal Reserve Act of 1913. It was, in effect, a compromise between proposals to either set up massive central banks or no central bank at all. The act provided for the establishment of a regional system of not less than eight or more than twelve reserve banks. Thus the fear that the new system would be dominated by the Money Trust was somewhat allayed. The act provided for federal government supervision of the twelve regional banks actually established but with capital and deposits supplied by member banks.

The division into twelve Federal Reserve districts and banks is usually justified by appeal to the economic argument that the country is too large and the activities of the different sections too diverse to encompass the entire country in a single region. Sections of the country with similar economic interests formed into single Federal Reserve districts to facilitate bank servicing of the region's economy. Politically, the division is justified by an appeal to democratic ideals. A single region and a single large central bank, so the argument goes, is contrary to the democratic ideals dominant in the United States since the overthrow of the first two Banks of the United States.

The concept of federal monetary authority has advanced since 1913, and reorganization of the Federal Reserve System, which occurred since the 1930s, is but a case in point. Powers of the central authority have increased. This development is not without mixed blessings. All too often the central authorities embraced many defunct monetary ideas including various manifestations of the "real bills" doctrine.

The centralized nature of the system is provided by the example of the ownership of the Federal Reserve Banks. The federal government is the "owner" of the Federal Reserve Banks and, in effect, of this system. A claim to the regional or decentralized nature of the system cannot be achieved by the line of argument that member banks "own" the system. The idea, popular with some people, that it is otherwise is a misconception derived from the fact that the law requires member banks to own "stock" in Federal Reserve Banks.

Instead of stock ownership, what really exists is a sort of forced contract under which a 6 percent rate of return is paid to member banks to participate in the public enterprise of money creation under rules imposed by the federal government. Although Federal Reserve stock is riskless and the 6 percent of return is generous, it is not an arrangement for the cooperation of equals but the indulgence of a superior—namely, the federal government.

By and large the new Federal Reserve System and its policies became dominated by Benjamin Strong from 1914 until his death in 1928. President Woodrow Wilson appointed Strong to the position of governor of the Federal Reserve Bank of New York in 1914, at the time the most powerful post in the Federal Reserve System. Milton Friedman and Anna J. Schwartz, in their study of monetary policy, discuss at length Strong's influence on the Federal Reserve and its policies as well as the mistakes and ineptitude of the Federal Reserve in the 1920s and 1930.[2] Many of these policies were decided by Strong without consulting or even against the wishes of the Federal Reserve Board in Washington.

The turbulent 1920s and the subsequent Great Depression revealed the wobbly structure of the American banking system. The large number of independent banks without adequate deposit insurance encouraged a domino effect when one bank failed. Depositors demanded their money from banks whose assets were frozen. The situation was not helped when the Federal Reserve system failed in its function as "lender of last resort." Again, the Federal Reserve System's mistakes, blunders, and "ineptitute" in the 1920s and 1930s are described by Milton Friedman and Anna J. Schwartz in their monetary history.

The Federal Reserve's errors began when it failed to tighten money in 1919, and were compounded when tight money was applied too late, too much, and for too long in 1920. To be sure the monetary authorities had an explanation for each. In 1919, monetary policy was still subordinate to U.S. Treasury needs. In 1920, when the gold reserve was under pressure, the rules of orthodox central banking and the gold standard called for tight money.

During the mid-1920s, the American money supply grew at more or less a regular rate, and the economy performed well. Toward the end of the 1920s, however, monetary errors came with increasing frequency. It was at this point that the Federal Reserve authorities made their biggest mistake by following a policy that was too easy to break the speculative boom and too tight to promote growth. This mistake was compounded by an exaggerated view of the importance of the stock market. Indeed, much more can be added about how the internecine squabble between the Federal Reserve Board and its New York bank inhibited effective measures to discourage speculation. Had the Federal Reserve authority exercised their ample powers they could have cut short the tragic process of monetary deflation and banking collapse, and they could have prevented the stock of money from contracting, thereby avoiding the successive liquidity crises.

As the depression wore on, more and more serious mistakes were made. Open-market purchases were entirely inadequate to turn the tide of deflation. Even worse, the monetary authorities, in order to protect the gold stock, made the unbelievable mistake of tightening money at the depth of the trough in October 1931 by raising the rediscount rate and by open-market sales.

Given the premises and philosophy underlying American monetary policy, the Federal Reserve System would sooner or later run into disaster. Except for Governor B. Strong, little attention was paid to the money stock by those who were formulating and executing monetary policy. The fact is that the overwhelming majority of the most respected and influential economists of the day believed wholeheartedly in the philosophy and policy that the Federal Reserve System followed in committing its worst mistakes. Orthodox monetary theorists were mesmerized by the gold standard, haunted by an almost pathological fear of inflation, shocked by amateur stock market speculation, and led astray by the "real bills" doctrine. When the bull market entered its most intense phase in 1927, orthodox theorists urged the Federal Reserve System to tighten money in order to eliminate speculative activity.

It is possible that the Federal Reserve's mistakes are indeed as some authors argue. In the process of protecting the economy from exaggerated dangers, policymakers may have blundered into economic disaster. Politically, economically, and perhaps psychologically, Americans had a very difficult time handling the Great Depression.

The climate of opinion has changed. The pursuit of fixed exchange rates and the gold standard has given way to a more sophisticated version of monetary theory. A significant body of theorists are now more likely to consider the stock of money as a more significant factor than hitherto. To them, the forces determining the long-run rate of growth of real income are largely independent of the long-run rate of growth in the stock of money so long as both proceed fairly smoothly; however, marked instability of money is accompanied by instability of economic growth. Friedman and Schwartz describe it well in their study when they say that money is "rather clearly the senior partner in longer-run movements and in major cyclical movements, and an equal partner in shorter-run and milder movements."

POLICY TOOLS

The Federal Reserve System has at its disposal primarily three tools to implement policy, all of which operate through the volume of reserves that member banks hold at their Federal Reserve banks. The three tools are the discount rate, which affects the cost of reserves; the reserve requirements, which determine the percentage of deposit liabilities that member banks must hold as reserves; and the open-market operations, which affects the volume of reserves.

Both the discount rate and discount policy have played an important role since the early years of the Federal Reserve as well as other central banks. The significance of both declined in the 1930s when a weak demand for credit and an inflow of gold resulted in banks accumulating large excess reserves. Their role was further downgraded during World War II and early postwar years, and the Federal Reserve policy of supporting the prices of U.S. Government securities thereby providing ready access for member banks to Reserve Bank credit. In effect, for the better part of two decades, little use was made of the so-called "discount window."

When the policy of supporting the prices of U.S. Government securities ended in 1951, discount rate and discount policy once again came into prominence. The "discount window" provides member banks a way to obtain funds to cover reserve deficiencies. Nevertheless, discount rate and discount policy are no longer as important as in earlier years.

The discount rate is the oldest tool at the disposal of central banks. It is closely linked to the oldest theory of central banking—the commercial-bills doctrine. In many countries the discount mechanism remains the most important tool for domestic monetary controls. Indeed, in some countries until recently it was the only significant tool available to the central bank.

While the discount rate affects the cost of credit, minimum reserve requirements affect its availability. Legal reserve requirements have emerged as a most important tool of monetary control, supplanting in several countries the importance of the discount rate.

Legal reserve requirements and the authority to vary them within given ranges provides the Federal Reserve System and other central banks a tool for controlling the base of deposit creation and so for the expansion (or contraction) of bank credit. First introduced in the United States, legal reserve requirements are now an important part of monetary powers in many countries.

A major policy tool for the Federal Reserve System is open-market operation used to cause member banks to adjust their supply of deposits and loans by creating or destroying the reserves available to support them. The Federal Reserve carries out such an operation by purchasing or selling U.S. government securities from dealers in the market for these instruments. Thus, when the Federal Reserve purchases securities, it pays for them by crediting the reserves of member banks in which dealers maintain accounts; on the other hand, member bank reserves are debited when the Federal Reserve sells securities. Effective use of open-market operations has thus far been limited to more advanced industrial countries where the depth and broadness of their money market make open-market operations feasible.

In the United States, open-market operations are the most commonly used tool by the Federal Reserve System. It has considerable flexibility both as to timing and the amount of funds released or absorbed. Policy is determined by the Federal Open Market Committee, but responsibility for executing the transaction is delegated to the manager of the open market account. The manager has the responsibility of carrying out policy as determined by the committee of making purchases and sales in the market to implement the committee's directive.

These then are three principle tools available to central banks and in our illustration the Federal Reserve System. To be sure other countries have also developed other tools to take account of their special institutional arrangements, such as minimum liquidity ratios (special reserve requirements), whereby in addition to cash certain government securities are included among the eligible reserve assets and so serve to immobilize a portion of commercial bank government securities portfolio. Other special tools include suggestions by government authorities that commercial banks restrain their lending activities to established loan ceilings as well as detailed administrative instructions covering bank assets and liabilities. In sum, the variability of tools and their use depend not only on a country's economic development and financial structure, but also on other socioeconomic and political policies in place as well as on the urgency of the problems to be solved within the country.

THE CLASSICAL GOLD STANDARD, MANAGED FIDUCIARY STANDARD, AND ECONOMIC PERFORMANCE SINCE THE NINETEENTH CENTURY

Insight into the performance of central banks in Great Britain and the United States can be gained by considering the performance of monetary regimes in place since 1834. Available evidence appears to suggest that economic performance in Great Britain and the United States was better under the classical gold standard than under the managed fiduciary standard. For instance, both the price level and real economic activity were more stable in the pre-1914 period under the gold standard than in any period since. The unfortunate coincidence of troubles which produced the collapse of the international monetary and financial framework, and the subsequent deflation, real output instability, and high unemployment that characterize the period account for much of the poor performance. These results underscore our earlier discussion of the profound political, philosophic, economic, and social changes that have occurred in the world since the early years of the twentieth century.

According to evidence presented by M. D. Bordo, a slight downtrend on the average of 0.14 percent per year in the price level is registered in the United States during the period 1834–1913.[3] The exceptions in this trend are the sharp price rises during the 1830s, substantial capital imports into the United States, and again price rises from 1861–1866 during the American Civil War when the United States was off the gold standard. The rapid price deflation from 1869 to 1890 was necessitated by an American return to the gold standard in 1879.

Price stability does not characterize the period since World War I. In fact, in the United Kingdom, the United States, and elsewhere, price levels have, on average, been rising. Short periods of price stability occurred during the 1920s under the gold exchange standard, the 1950s, and the early 1960s under the Bretton Woods regime. For the period 1914–1979, price levels in the United States registered an annual rate of increase of 2.2 percent and for the United Kingdom an average annual increase of 3.81 percent.

Overall the record does indicate more long-term price stability during the gold standard era than in the years since departure from that standard. The tendency for price levels to revert toward long-run stable value under the gold standard ensured a measure of predictability with respect to the value of money. There could be short-term price rises or declines; inflation or deflation, however, would not continue.

Long-term price stability encouraged people to enter into contracts on the expectation that changes in prices for commodities and factors of production would reflect real changes and not changes in the value of money brought about by inflation or deflation. One consequence of departure from the gold standard and lack of constraint in general prices is to generate confusion, as between changes in price levels and changes in relative prices. This confusion increases the possibility for people to misjudge market signals and so incur major economic losses.

The evidence on real per capita income for the United States and the United Kingdom suggests that it was more stable under the gold standard than in any period since World War I. For the United States the mean absolute value of percentage deviations of real per capita income from trend is 6.64 percent from 1879 to 1913, and 8.97 percent from 1919 to 1979 (excluding 1941–1945). There is, moreover, in the United Kingdom a permanent break in trend in 1919, so that in subsequent years real per capita income is almost always below trend.

Unemployment, too, is on average lower in the pre-1914 period in both the United States and the United Kingdom than in the post–World War I period. For the United States, average unemployment for 1890–1919 is 6.78 percent. For the United Kingdom the average unemployment rate over the period 1888–1913 is 4.30 percent, and for the period 1919–1979 (excluding the World War II years 1939–1945) it is 6.42 percent.

The evidence thus tends to support the view that the classical gold standard is associated with more economic stability than the managed fiduciary regime by which it was replaced. The problem with the comparison is that it includes the interwar period when the international monetary and financial organizations collapsed.

The evidence presented by M. D. Bordo takes this into account. Accordingly, three time periods are compared: the pre–World War I gold standard period, the interwar period, and the post–World war II period. In point of fact, both world war years are omitted for comparison. Overall prices are more variable under the gold standard than in both post-gold standard periods. The least variability occurs in the post–World War II period. For the United States, average annual percentage change in prices for the period 1879–1913 is 0.1 percent, and the coefficient of variation of annual percentage changes in the price level is 17.0. For the United Kingdom during the period 1870–1913 prices drift downward at an annual percentage change of −0.7 percent and a coefficient of variation of −14.9. For the period 1919–1940 the U.S. records an annual percentage change in price of 2.5 percent with a coefficient of variation of −5.2. For the United Kingdom and the period 1919–1938, the average annual percentage change in prices is −4.6 percent with a coefficient of variation of 3.8. The post–World War II years 1946–1979 for the United States showed an average annual percentage rise in the price level of 2.8 percent with a coefficient of variation of 1.3. For the United Kingdom the average annual percentage rise in prices is 5.6 percent with a coefficient of variation of 1.2.

The stability of real output is suggested by the coefficient of variation of year-to-year changes in real per capita output. The evidence suggests for the United States a coefficient of variation of 3.5 for the period 1879–1913; 5.5 for the period 1919–1940; 1.6 for the period 1946–1979. For the United Kingdom this coefficient is 2.5 for the period 1919–1938; 1.4 for the period 1946–1979. In sum, real output is considerably less stable in both countries during the interwar years to the post–World War

II years in both countries when higher rates of inflation and lower variability in output and employment are registered. It demonstrates the apparent policy preference away from long-term price stability toward full employment and suggests the reason, described earlier, behind the strong inflationary pressures in the postwar years. It is on the basis of such evidence that the public recognized that a specie or gold standard–like monetary regime no longer existed and began to arrange their affairs accordingly.

The evidence also suggests that a fiduciary money standard based on a monetary rule for steady monetary growth could provide the benefits of the gold standard without its costs. A prerequisite for success, however, is a firm commitment on the part of government to maintain a monetary rule as well as to incorporate as one of its goals long-run price stability.

In any case, the fact is that the international specie or gold standard cannot be restored. It requires a return to the set of economic, political, and philosophic beliefs upon which that standard is based and which we have discussed. This is unlikely. It is probably easier to deprive the government altogether of its monopoly over money. The magnitude of such a task, however, should not be minimized. The sensitive issue of national sovereignty is involved. For this reason, among others we have discussed, governments will not voluntarily abdicate their power over money.

NOTES

1. See George Macesich, *Commercial Banking and Regional Development in the United States, 1950–1960* (Tallahassee: Florida State University Press, 1965).

2. For an analysis of the period preceding and following the establishment of the Federal Reserve System see Milton Friedman and Anna J. Schwartz, *A Monetary History of the United States 1867–1960* (New York: National Bureau of Economic Research and Princeton University Press, 1963).

3. See M. D. Bordo, "The Classical Gold Standard: Some Lessons for Today." *Monthly Review* (Federal Reserve Bank of St. Louis, May 1981): 2–17.

Chapter 5

Central Banking and Bureaucracy

CENTRAL BANKS AND THE THEORY OF BUREAUCRACY

Central bankers cannot be expected to take seriously any theory or empirical evidence that would strive to constrain their activities. This has little to do with individual central bankers, many of whom are outstanding. At issue here is the system itself, the bureaucracy, and the incentives that central bankers respond to.

Central banks as government agencies exercise discretionary policy. It is thus important to base an independent evaluation of their performance in terms of explicit criteria. Central bankers are loath to accept the constraint, because they view the exercise of monetary policy as an art that cannot be defined or measured by any single variable. They prefer to discuss monetary policy in unmeasured variables, such as the intuition of policymakers, as the state of monetary restraint in terms of a set of non-equivalent measuring variables among which the interpreter is free to choose at will. We draw on recent American experience to illustrate and underscore the issues involved.

Congress passed Concurrent Resolution 133 in 1995, which stated that the Federal Reserve should control monetary aggregates and consult with and report to Congress at regular intervals. This was a resolution strongly opposed by the Federal Reserve Board. When passed, the Federal Reserve pledged cooperation; however, within two years, the Federal Reserve had undermined the resolution.[1]

If Congress had not been able to bend the Federal Reserve to its will, a study by Beck suggests that past presidents had been more successful.[2] It is argued that since the Treasury–Federal Reserve Accord of March 1951, American presidents have been the principal political influence behind Federal Reserve policy. According to evidence cited in the study, Federal Reserve policy was significantly changed in all the years in which the presidency changed. This is consistent with our theory: Risk avoidance would push the Federal Reserve to pay closer attention to presidential desires than those of Congress. It is the president and his administration that can directly threaten the Federal Reserve's status as an agency. First, the president has the power to name the chairman of the Federal Reserve Board and at least two other members of the board during each presidential term. There is, moreover, a close working relationship between the administration and the Federal Reserve Board. The notable exception is Alan Greenspan. According to Washington observers, George Bush blamed Greenspan for Bush's defeat because Greenspan failed to reduce interest rates in 1991. Bill Clinton was also annoyed when Greenspan raised interest rates in 1994.

It is significant that during the important monetary policy changes between 1950 and 1970, the same individual, William M. Martin, was chairman. The strong presidential influence under which the central bankers of the Federal Reserve operate is suggested by events during the tenure of President Lyndon B. Johnson (1963–1969). There are also the years when market participants began to realize that significant changes were occurring in the country's monetary regime away from a constrained gold (specie) standard–like regime to an unconstrained government fiat standard.

Additional confirmation of presidential influence on the Federal Reserve is provided by the Nixon administration (1969–1974), when Arthur Burns served as chairman. In 1972, when Nixon was running for reelection, the old M1 (currency plus demand deposits) definition of the money supply grew at almost 8.5 percent during the last quarter of 1972 and the first quarter of 1973, or at better than 6 percent during the period 1969–1974. This is indeed a postwar record growth in the money supply. President Richard Nixon also removed the country's last links with gold in 1971. To this may be added the administration's futile attempt to hold down inflation by wage and price controls while simultaneously promoting an expansive monetary supply.

President Jimmy Carter at first considered inflation a monetary phenomenon and promoted monetary growth in order to lower interest rates and encourage investment. Arthur Burns continued to serve as the Federal Reserve chairman until March 1978, when Carter appointed G. William Miller to the position. In November 1978, President Carter changed priorities, from stimulating the economy to fighting inflation, which had spurted into double digits. From the previous high of an over 8.5 percent rate of growth in old M1 reached by October 1978, the money supply growth was slowed by March 1979. Thereafter, it took off again with the M1 growing at a 13 percent annual rate between March and October 1979.

Paul Volcker became chairman of the Federal Reserve in August 1979. On October 6, 1979, he announced that the Federal Reserve would henceforth concentrate on directly controlling the money supply and deemphasize interest rates as targets. Indeed comments by President Ronald Reagan suggest that it might be a good idea to put the Federal Reserve under Treasury supervision underscoring disappointment with the Federal Reserve's performance.

It should be expected that an agency such as the Federal Reserve would push its own version of history. Such activities might range from outright concealment of information that could be unfavorable to it or helpful to its critics, to favoring a general framework in which agency activities would be interpreted so as to minimize any interpretation that it had made any serious errors.

On this score, it is interesting to note that the Federal Reserve undertook an extensive examination of its experience with monetary aggregates. In a two volume study, the conclusion reached was that "the basic operating procedure represents a sound approach to attaining long-run objectives set for monetary standards."[3]

A BOTTOM LINE?

Quite a few observers will agree with Milton Friedman when he writes, "I believe that the fundamental explanation of bureaucratic inertia in the Federal Reserve System is the absence of a bottom line."[4] In short, the Federal Reserve operates in a manner consistent with the theory of bureaucracy. This realization has prompted more fundamental proposals for monetary reform.

Perceptive scholars have long called attention to the emergence of a new class, which they have called either bureaucratic or managerial. In this view, neither capitalists nor politicians were really running things. Instead, on the basis of expertise, a new group had insinuated itself into power everywhere, and the enormity and complexity of the tasks confronting contemporary society served to promote the interests of this group.

These issues have prompted scholars to increasingly devote their talents to searching for what must be done to overhaul and direct the state and its bureaucracy to more effectively serve the desires and interests of its electorate. Thought must be given to designing intelligent and rational constraints to the exercise of arbitrary power by both the bureaucracy of the state and large autonomous organizations. It is counterproductive to heap abuse, contempt, and new tasks on these groups without a clear idea of what the "rules of the game" are for their behavior.

In this study and in others, I have turned to cooperation theory, the theory of public choice, and economics for helpful insights into bureaucratic and political behavior.[5] According to public choice theory, politicians and bureaucrats are just like other people, driven chiefly by egocentricity, not altruism. The theory teaches, for instance, that because politicians respond to pressure groups and the desire to be reelected, the actions of government will often create or magnify market imperfections rather than overcome them. From this, the theory's followers tend to argue, logically, that the actions of government should be limited. Thus, the popularity among public choice theorists is of first, a constitutional amendment to require a balanced budget; second, deregulation; and, third, as recommended in this study, a system of well-defined guidelines within a lawful policy system of rules to constrain the monetary authority's discretionary monetary policy.

Of course, not everyone is prepared to accept the implications of the economic model for the behavior of the bureaucracy and political elite. In particular, they are not prepared to accept the constraints on discretionary decision making by the bureaucracy. They argue that such impediments as distinguishing facts from values, the ambiguous nature of goals, and the pressures and costs of information acquisition cast doubt on constraining discretionary authority. In any case, some argue that goals cannot, and should not, be agreed upon in advance of decisions.

Critics note that political and economic choices are often formulated in different terms and directed toward fulfilling different kinds of objectives and should, therefore, be evaluated by different criteria. For example,

Aaron Wildavsky suggests that in a political setting a bureaucracy's need for political support assumes central importance, and that political costs and benefits of decisions are critical.[6] However, these costs and benefits are very difficult to measure and quantify. According to Wildavsky, political benefits that might accrue to a bureaucracy might be evident enough—but the political costs might be less obvious and would need explicit categorization.

Wildavsky suggests the use of "exchange costs," which are incurred when the bureaucracy or the politically elite need the support of other groups or people. For example, "hostility costs" may be incurred when a politician antagonizes a group of people and may suffer their retaliation. These hostility costs may mount and become "election costs," which in turn may become "policy costs" through the inability to command the necessary formal powers to accomplish the desired policy objectives. He also suggests "reputation costs" arising from the loss of esteem and effectiveness with other participants in the political system and the loss of ability to secure policies other than those under immediate review.

It is also possible, as we have seen, that bureaucracies tend to behave for political reasons, as suggested by Anthony Downs.[7] Thus, he describes a group of decision makers as "conservers" whose cautious behavior to minimize individual or institutional risks is inherently political. Self-interest motives, which Downs assigns to "climbers" as well as "conservers," are themselves political. Only Down's primarily altruistic "statesman" seems to have the general good, not politics, in view. However, Downs suggests that by not contesting for organizational resources, the statesman's function will simply be underfunded.

In effect, most decisions that are measured have political implications because of the ever present possibility that adherence to a particular set of criteria will ultimately favor the political interests of one group over those of other groups. Indeed, caution must be exercised to avoid both the unthinking application of economic criteria to the measurement of political phenomena and the assumption that the economic rationality is, by definition, superior to political rationality.

Advocates of political rationality defend it on the following grounds: (1) one can accept the proposition that politics is legitimately concerned with enabling the decision processes of government to function adequately; (2) basing decisions on political grounds is as valid as basing them on other grounds; (3) according to the currency of politics, political rationality is as defensible as rationality in economic terms. Properly conceived and applied, political rationality can be a useful means for gaining insight into bureaucratic processes.

Traditional conceptions of bureaucracy and its role in government are not altogether accurate. Nevertheless, these conceptions are important in shaping views on bureaucracy. They include political neutrality in carrying out the decisions of other government organizations; legislative intent as a principal guiding force for the actions of bureaucracy as a legitimate corollary to legislative intent; and directions by the chief executive, which creates possibilities for conflict over the control of bureaucracy in a system of separation of powers.

In the United States significant problems exist because of the fragmented nature of the various policy-making processes.[8] The American bureaucracy functions in a political environment where no central control over policy exists; consequently, there is considerable slack in the system that allows the bureaucracy considerable disorientation. Moreover, not all decision-making power or authority is clearly allocated, resulting in many small conflicts over fragments of power. The net result is that American bureaucrats are often active in political roles and take policy initiatives that are not neutral, thereby departing from traditional views about bureaucratic roles and functions. They are, in effect, in a position to develop semi-independence from elected leaders. Furthermore, their activity is organized around jurisdiction over particular policy across, for example, Federal Reserve, monetary policy, and banking. Finally, they make a special effort to prevent changes in jurisdiction that might affect their political interests or those of their supporters, for example, the Federal Reserve and its relations with federal and local authorities in monetary and banking affairs.

This study focuses on bureaucratic power and accountability in contemporary society. Bureaucratic power is mostly based on the ability to build, retain, and mobilize political support for a given agency and its programs, and to make use of expertise in certain affairs, such as monetary and banking affairs by the Federal Reserve. Bureaucratic accountability, especially in the United States, is difficult to enforce with consistency and effectiveness because of the frequency of conflicting interests in the legislative and executive branches of government. The issue of accountability is made all the more difficult because American bureaucracies operate under authority delegated by both the chief executive and the legislative branch, with considerable discretion to make independent choices.

As has been noted, bureaucratic power rests on adequate political support and expertise in the programs being administered. The sources of political support are various legislative and executive committees, staffs, and clientele groups whose interests are closely associated with the operation of the agency itself. The political impact of agency expertise, or near-expertise, on issues involved serves to reinforce its power.

In addition to being accountable to government and the people the bureaucracy is also accountable to its clientele groups, which in turn may reduce accountability to the larger political system. Other means of accountability include judicial decisions, public exposure, and the news media. However, in the final analysis, bureaucracies are accountable to those with power to make them do so. No other impact on bureaucracies is as pronounced. Accountability is a product of politics, and it is best achieved and maintained through the political process. Widespread dissatisfaction with an agency's performance can have an effect. A case in point was the public outcry against both the upswing in inflation in the 1970s and Federal Reserve policies.

Both Max Weber's concern with bureaucracy and his contribution to its conceptual development have served to shape subsequent views of bureaucracy.[9] He was the first to define systematically the dimension of this new form of social organization and to prescribe or explain its operations in abstract and theoretical terms. In his view, a government bureaucracy should be endowed with sufficient legal and political authority to function adequately. He saw it as an ideal-type form of organization as it emerged within the European experience—a broad framework rather than an all-encompassing model.

A good illustration of bureaucracy in operation in the central banking field is provided by Alan Greenspan, chairman of the Federal Reserve since the mid-1980s into the early 2000s. Considered a successful central banker and economist he has managed to gain the confidence of many people. Indeed, his reputation is such that some people would be quite willing to accept the idea that the American dollar backed by Federal Reserve Board chairman Alan Greenspan is just as good as one backed by gold.[10] Apparently, few people fear that Chairman Greenspan's successor might resemble G. William Miller, Federal Reserve Board chairman in the late 1970s who seemed to have no idea how to slow inflation.

There are studies that examine a monetary regime wherein the reputation of monetary authorities is substituted for formal rules.[11] The difficulty with such a regime is the potential for multiple equilibria. Thus, if people base future beliefs on the policymaker's reputation and actions, the policymaker may be motivated to validate these beliefs. It is difficult to ascertain how the economy would settle on an equilibria that tends to generate the best overall results. In any case, an analysis that relies on differences in the personal characteristics of policymakers (e.g., Greenspan and those who will follow) leaves little scope for systematic economic analysis.

Still, reputation does seem to prevail in many areas of public policy and so may be superior to a formal rule. Nevertheless, it is far easier to establish a "bottom line" for bureaucracies including central banks by formal rules supported by appropriate enforcement mechanisms than on discretionary authority dependent on the personal characteristics of present and future policymakers. In any case, it may be desirable to consider the costs of establishing and enforcing formal rules against the results delivered by reputation and discretionary authority.

NOTES

1.   See Milton Friedman, "Monetary Policy: Theory and Practice," *Journal of Money, Credit, and Banking* (February 1982): 108.

2.   See Nathaniel Beck, "Presidential Influence on the Federal Reserve in the 1970s," *American Journal of Political Science* (August 1982): 415–445.

3.   *New Monetary Control Procedures*, Federal Reserve Staff Study, Vols. 1 and 2 (Washington, D.C.: Board of Governors of the Federal Reserve System, February 1982).

4.   Friedman, "Monetary Policy: Theory and Practice," p. 124.

5.   See George Macesich, *Economic Nationalism and Stability* (New York: Praeger, 1985), pp. 11–21.

6.   Aaron Wildavsky, *The Politics of the Budgetary Process*, 2nd ed. (Boston: Little Brown, 1974), pp. 11–21.

7.   See Anthony Downs, *Inside Bureaucracy* (Boston: Little Brown, 1967) chap.

8.   See George J. Gordon, *Public Administration in America*, 2nd ed. (New York: St. Martin's Press, 1982), Chap. 1.

9.   Max Weber, *On Charisma and Institutions Building—Selected Papers*, edited with an introduction by S. M. Eisonstadt (Chicago: University of Chicago Press, 1968).

10.   See, for example, Floyd Norris, "Greenspan Has Become the New Gold Standard," *International Herald Tribune*, May 4, 1999: 11.

11.   See, for instance, Robert J. Barro and Davis B. Gordon, "A Positive Theory of Monetary Policy in a Natural Rate Model," *Journal of Political Economy*, August 1983: 589–610; Phillip Cagan, "Financial Developments and the Erosion of Monetary Controls," in *Contemporary Economic Problems*, William Fellner, ed. (Washington, D.C.: American Enterprise Institute for Public Policy,

1979), pp. 117–151; David Kreps and Robert Wilson, "Reputations and Imperfect Information," *Journal of Economic Theory*, August 1982: 253–279.

Chapter 6

Monetary Policy

A CHANGING ENVIRONMENT

Monetary policy is understood to mean actions taken by central banks (and monetary authorities) to affect monetary and other financial conditions for the purpose of broader objectives such as price stability, high employment, and sustainable growth of real output.

The influence of monetary authorities through central bank operations has changed markedly from even so recent a period as the 1970s and 1980s. The so-called transmission mechanism of the 1990s through which monetary policy influences the general economy is but a case in point. For instance, the Federal Reserve System (Fed) has the most influence over short-term interest rates through its federal funds rate. This is the rate that banks pay one another for overnight borrowing. Thus the Fed announces a target federal funds rate and then influences movements in this rate by buying government securities from or selling them to banks. A higher federal funds rate promotes a rise in other short-term interest rates as banks pass their increased funding costs on to their customers.

The standard explanation argues that as the nominal interest rate rises but people's expectations of inflation stay the same, real interest rates will rise. The effect is an increase in the cost of borrowing and the return on savings and thus a fall in consumption and investment. The economy slows down and inflationary pressure is eased.

Another channel through which monetary policy operates is the wealth effect. In this instance higher interest rates mean that future revenue from such assets as equities must be discounted higher than the earlier rate. As a consequence, the holders of such assets now feel poorer and so they spend less. At the same time, a fall in the market value of existing firms makes it less expensive to acquire new assets' by buying existing firms rather than buying new equipment. The net result is to lower investment expenditures.

Exchange rates are also influenced by changes in interest rates. Thus, a rise in interest rates, other things equal, will tend to appreciate a country's currency. On balance, the appreciating-currency country will find its exports more expensive, resulting in a slowdown in domestic output.

Other observers cite bank practices that can be altered by central bank action. For instance, banks may well respond to a tighter monetary policy by raising their loan rates while at the same time reducing the number of their loans.

It is the financial markets, however, that have recently gained in significance as a channel through which monetary policy operates. Central bank operations do indeed alter financial market expectations about future inflation rates. The financial markets may well be convinced by central bank action to raise short-term rates and that the bank is serious about controlling inflation and so limit any increase in long-term rates. Given that bond yields, for instance, adjust very quickly to financial and other sensitive rates, capital markets can more rapidly reinforce central bank action than ordinary banks.

The relationship between financial markets and central banks, however, rests on resolutely controlling inflation. In effect, a central bank with credibility and a strong anti-inflationary record can cut financial market expectations regarding inflation much quicker and so squeeze inflation at a smaller cost in terms of the economy's output and unemployment. Central bank credibility is the basic ingredient for carrying out a successful policy of controlling inflation.

Indeed, in the 1990s inflation in the industrial countries has averaged 3.5 percent, compared with 6 percent a year in the 1980s.[1] Long-term rates have fallen as well, from 10 percent to 7.2 percent. Expectations of inflation have gone down. At the same time, the credibility of many central banks as inflationary pressures are eased has increased. Clearly, if central banks and monetary authorities can preserve their credibility as inflation fighters, their policies may well work quicker, due to the growing influence of financial markets in shaping the effect of monetary policy.

Various countries have experienced different impacts in their monetary policy channels. For instance, in the United States, Germany, and Italy, the effect on banks' lending rates of a one-percentage-point rise in the official short-term interest rate fell sharply between 1975–1989 and 1990–1996, which suggests that the traditional transmission mechanism has lost some of its force. Japan and Canada, on the other hand, register a modest rise.

Other evidence suggests that stock market capitalization has grown far faster than banks' liabilities, measured by broad-money aggregates in, for example, the United States, Sweden, and France. An implication of such a development is that in these three countries, banks have become less important conductors of monetary policy. In Japan, however, the importance of banks in the transmission mechanism has risen. In a number of other European countries the relative importance of banking has remained constant.

It may be that the relative effectiveness of monetary channels is changing; monetary policy, however, has lost none of its overall potency. Indeed, for many countries for which results are available, a rise in short-term interest rates has a stronger and quicker effect on output in the 1990s than it did in the 1970s and 1980s. Again, the growing importance of financial markets in shaping the effect of monetary policy is growing. An important result is that central bankers can expect that their policies may well work faster in the future, provided that they can achieve and preserve credibility in preserving price stability and so controlling inflation.

IMPORTANCE OF CREDIBILITY

Achieving and preserving credibility on the part of central banks and monetary authorities is indeed critical. Some observers argue that the monetary authorities actually limit the scope of their discretion by adhering to a fairly restrictive rule or set of rules governing the determination of the money. Indeed, the type of behavior necessary to convince the public of the authorities' determination could most likely resemble a nondiscretionary path. The fact is that a major difficulty in designing an optimal monetary arrangement is that we do not know enough about the rate at which the credibility of monetary authorities is eroded by the exercise of discretionary power.

Concern over the credibility of monetary authorities has prompted recent examinations of the history of the gold standard and proposals that the United States return to such a standard.[2] The appeal of the gold standard is its presumed tendency toward a predictable long-run value of the monetary unit. Unlike the gold standard, the U.S. government is committed to keeping the price of gold fixed and is willing to convert the dollar into gold at a fixed price. Such an arrangement requires the Treasury to maintain gold reserves sufficient for the volume of sales that may be necessary to peg the price of gold, and of course the Treasury is obligated to sell gold whenever the price of gold rises. Clearly any attempt to conduct discretionary monetary policy that would threaten the price of gold is ruled out.

Of course the predictable long-run value of the monetary unit depends on the predictability of the increase in the supply of gold. For the price level to maintain a constant long-run value, the long-run supply of gold would have to be perfectly elastic. Under less elastic gold supply conditions, the price level would fluctuate around a long-run deflationary trend. If the cost of producing gold is subject to shocks such as discoveries of new ore deposits or technological improvements in the extraction process, the long-run predictability of the price level may be significantly reduced.

In any case, Anna Schwartz points out that the embrace of the gold standard by the United States as a way to constrain the exercise of discretionary monetary management is not likely in the near future. Such a change in monetary arrangements would require dramatic changes that Americans are not likely to accept. It is not at all certain, moreover, that prices would actually be more predictable.

Characteristics of commodity standards in general, including the gold standard, were discussed by Milton Friedman several decades ago.[3] Their shortcomings and disadvantages and advantages as monetary standards were discussed in detail by Friedman. Suffice it here to underscore, as he does, that commodity standards do have certain automatic characteristics as well as freedom from political control provided that the commodity (e.g., gold) is the only means for changing the supply of money. Any such arrangement would require a steady accumulation of commodity stocks so as to provide for secular growth of the stock of money. As a consequence, significant resources are necessary to acquire the necessary stock of money. Any attempt to reduce the costs of such an operation will very likely involve political intervention and control—and, of course, also provide an incentive for the introduction of fiat money.

Moreover, successful international operations of such commodity standards as gold that would produce stable exchange rates requires that countries be willing to permit complete free trade in gold and submit their internal monetary and economic policies to its discipline. Clearly, this is not likely in the contemporary world economy.

It is not surprising that the U.S. Gold Commission in 1982 failed to endorse an important role for gold in American monetary arrangements. The collapse of the post–World War II Bretton Woods system along with the special role of the United States and the dollar ended operation of a gold-centered monetary system. There is no evidence that other countries are interested in the gold standard.

There is little doubt of the importance of credibility and cooperation of politicians and bureaucrats responsible for domestic and international economic policies, including monetary policy in particular. Past experience underscores that central banks cannot fine-tune the economy and that in trying to do so they may jeopardize the goal of price stability. In their eagerness to boost growth and so keep politicians happy, many central banks, including the Federal Reserve System, cast in doubt their own credibility before the public at large.

In the American case, the blame lies primarily with Congress for giving the Federal Reserve the contradictory goals of promoting growth and constraining inflation. The Bank of Canada is more subject to political manipulation than the Federal Reserve, at least on paper, nonetheless it is in practice freer to pursue price stability. Explicit price targets make easier the Bank of Canada's tasks of promoting its credibility and so helping to reduce inflationary expectations.

Even so, the Bank of Canada's job would be made easier, according to some observers, if like the Reserve Bank of New Zealand in 1990, it was also made freely independent of the government. Financial markets, to judge from a dramatic drop in interest rates, are giving the Reserve Bank good marks for credibility to stabilize prices.

There is growing support for the view that price level stability, popularly called *zero inflation*, is superior to inflation rate stability.[4] A contrary view is that the benefits of being at zero inflation are small compared to the costs of getting there, and that most of the costs associated with nonzero average rates of inflation can be adequately addressed by adopting institutional changes that do not require specific inflation targets.

Many analysts think that reducing price level uncertainty is a very desirable objective despite the apparent lack of evidence that such uncertainty has important social welfare costs. It is the long-run uncertainty of inflation that many analysts are concerned with and that makes the goal of zero price inflation so attractive to many of them.

In effect, the essential issue, even for skeptics of price stability, is that some type of rule is more desirable than none, including one for a specific low rate of inflation that would eliminate the distortions currently endured by uncertainty about future policy and future inflation trends.

GOALS, INDICATORS, AND TARGETS OF MONETARY POLICY

The formulation and execution of monetary policy very much depends on the philosophic, political, and economic views that monetary authorities and their political superiors hold. Especially important are their views on the role and importance of money in the economy, as discussed elsewhere in this study.

Monetary policy as it is usually understood by economists and others deals with objectives, tools, and processes in the regulation of the supply of money. It is argued that monetary policy primarily influences the value and composition of assets. As a result, it is more circuitous than, for example, fiscal policy, which directly influences income and therefore economic activity. A contrary position is that decisions regarding the demand to hold money really involve a decision about whether it is best to hold wealth in this form or in securities or physical assets. Against such a background, asset holdings may be as significant as income in directly influencing economic activity. Monetary policy, through its effect of assets, may theoretically have as direct an impact on economic activity as fiscal policy operating through income.[5]

Monetarists, or quantity theorists who place emphasis on the important role of money in economic activity, argue that the monetary authority can control nominal quantities of its own liabilities. By manipulating these quantities, it can fix the exchange rate, the nominal level of income, and the nominal quantity of money.[6] It can also directly influence the rate of inflation or deflation, the rate of growth of the nominal stock or money, and the rate of growth or decline in nominal national income. The monetary authority cannot, through control of nominal quantities, fix real quantities such as the real interest rate, the rate of unemployment, the level of real national income, the real quantity of money, nor can it fix the rate of growth of those quantities.

Economists are quick to point out, however, that this does not mean that monetary policy does not have important effects on these real magnitudes. Indeed, when money gets out of order, repercussions are felt throughout the economy. Monetary history provides ample evidence on this point. In fact, the long debate among economists and monetarists—led by Milton Friedman and the Keynesians—over the effectiveness of use of governmental monetary and fiscal policies to influence economic activity, provides us with a valuable example. Keynesians have argued that money and monetary policy have little or no impact on income and unemployment, particularly during severe economic depressions. Moreover, government spending and taxation (i.e., fiscal policy) are most effective when dealing with inflation and unemployment problems. Monetarists including Friedman have stressed the importance of money. They argue that a rule requiring the monetary authority to cause the nominal stock of money to increase by a fixed percentage annually would effectively reduce fluctuations in prices, real output, and employment.

It is thus generally agreed that by goals of monetary policy we mean ultimate aims or objectives, that is, price stability, economic growth, "full" or maximum employment, and balance of payments equilibrium. These are objectives shared by most countries.

When viewed individually, each of these goals appears straightforward. It is another matter, however, to achieve all of these goals at the same time. Conflicts arise. Reaching one goal may make it impossible to reach another. Then, the closer an economy is to full (or maximum) employment, the faster prices may rise. Under a system of fixed exchange rates, the balance of payments equilibrium requires that the domestic economy be systematically inflated and deflated. Moreover, the goal of economic growth may conflict with any or all these other goals. It is useful, therefore, to distinguish between a necessary conflict and a policy conflict.

A necessary conflict is one where the achievement of one goal necessarily means that another will not be achieved. An example of this is suggested by past arguments over the Phillips curve analysis, where a presumed trade-off occurs between full employment and price stability. An example of a policy conflict is when monetary policy cannot pursue both price stability and economic growth at the same time. Evidence suggests that a given rate of economic growth is consistent with a given rate of price increase. Countries have also experienced potential conflicts. Thus, except for price stability, monetarists argue that the achievement of other goals by monetary policy manipulation is an illusion.

Given the goals of monetary policy, it is necessary to design a strategy for their achievement. In essence, monetary policy strategy with explicit goals or objectives, intermediate targets, and operating targets must be available to the monetary authority. For the success of any given monetary strategy, it must have policy instruments to operate targets that, in turn, affect the intermediate targets that change the ultimate goal variables. At the same time, a useful monetary strategy must also have a method to monitor its effects on the economy.

Intermediate targets include monetary aggregates, credit aggregates, and capital market interest rates. Operating targets consist of such variables as bank reserve aggregates, money market conditions so indicated by the Treasury bill rate, free reserves, and, in the United States, the federal funds rate.

The monetary authorities cannot manipulate the money supply as directly as tax rates, nor can they determine the full structure of interest rates. As a result, they must often choose a particular operating target that is easier to manipulate with the instruments available but whose relationship to a particular intermediate target is reasonably well observed. Ready examples are the monetary base (i.e., currency plus the banking system's total reserves) in Switzerland and Italy. Short-term money market interest rates are traditional operating targets in the United Kingdom and Austria. In the past, total bank credit has been preferred as an operating target in France. In Germany, some ratio of bank liquidity has been used. In the Netherlands and Spain this ratio has usually meant the difference between some compulsory ratio of assets to liabilities and the actual ratio.

In essence, the distinction between the operating and intermediate targets varies from country to country. The choice of operating target depends mainly on the monetary instruments available to the country's monetary authorities. Indeed, the distinction between instruments and targets may well be very narrow. For example, the central bank discount rate is an instrument, whereas short-term interest rates as a whole are an operating target. Moreover, the instruments available depend very much on the country's financial structure.

There are at least six categories of instruments that are important. One is central bank transactions in securities. If a well-developed money and capital system exists, central banks can influence interest rates by buying and selling securities (usually government securities). These open market operations must be legitimate. They conflict, however, with a central bank's efforts on behalf of debt management operations for the government.

The second category is a central bank's lending operation. The way central bank lending operates depends on the country and the level of commercial bank indebtedness. In the United Kingdom, for instance, the central bank does not lend directly to commercial banks. It carries out its operations with the discount houses. In other countries the level of commercial bank indebtedness tends to be high—in France, for example. In any case, a central bank, in its capacity as lender of last resort, has a special role to play.

The third category of instruments concerns changes in minimum reserve requirements. Again, differences exist among countries. Reserve requirements may be fixed against all deposits or only against special kinds of deposits, as in Switzerland. Some central banks, such as in Geneva and France, have tended in the past to make frequent changes in reserve requirements.

The fourth category is controls on bank lending. Many countries use direct controls in some form.

The fifth category is direct control over interest rates. There is a trend toward eliminating such direct controls in most industrial countries. Nevertheless, changes in the discount rate as a signal to change their own rates.

The final category is controls on the foreign transactions of banks in response to foreign exchange movements. These controls are, in essence, manifestations of the above categories. More straightforward controls prohibit certain classes of transactions abroad or create special exchange rates for such transactions.

Many economists, especially monetarists, have a preference for a monetary aggregate target rather than a money market target as the appropriate target for monetary policy because it is closely associated with their view of the control of nominal and real rates of interest. Thus, monetarists hold that the authorities are best able to fix the nominal rate of interest. Their theory on the real rate of interest emphasizes the importance of the link between the nominal market rate of interest and the real rate of interest. Only if the expected rate of inflation is zero will nominal and real rates of interest be equal.

Furthermore, the choice in selecting a monetary aggregate target or money market target is conditioned on the relative importance of random disturbances occurring from the real and monetary sides of the economy. If the real side of the economy is more unstable, then a money aggregate target is preferable. If the monetary side of the economy is more unstable, then an interest rate target is preferable. However, the rate of interest relevant to expenditure decisions and therefore the position of the IS curve (in the IS-LM curve [Investment and Savings-Liquidity Money] for a closed economy) is the real rate of interest that the authorities cannot fix in any case.

The choice of an indicator that will quickly and accurately give the direction and magnitude of monetary policy is also closely associated with the monetarist preference for a monetary target. A useful indicator must possess such characteristics as a high degree of correlation with the target variables. Accurate and reliable statistics on the indicator must be quickly available to authorities, and the indicator should be exogenous rather then endogenous—that is, monetary authorities should be capable of controlling the variable. Indeed, Anna J. Schwartz eliminates the distinction between targets and indicators.[7] The ideal target, Schwartz argues, ought to be judged on three criteria: (1) Is it measurable? (2) Is it subject to control by central banks? (3) Is it a reliable indicator of monetary conditions? On the basis of data for the United Kingdom, Canada, and Japan, Schwartz concludes that the money stock is the best "target indicator." A similar conclusion is reached in other studies.[8]

The money supply and its sensitivity to interest rates in several countries has been studied.[9] Together, with other studies, there is now a considerable amount of empirical evidence on the interest sensitivity of some reserve multipliers. If these multipliers are highly sensitive to interest rate changes, then it may be difficult to implement monetary control through reserve aggregates, but to judge from the evidence so far, the interest sensitivity of various multipliers is low. Accordingly, control of monetary aggregates through reserves does not present a serious problem.

Alternative approaches to monetary control are not always satisfactory. Thus, criticism of Alan Greenspan, chairman of the Federal Reserve Board of Governors, for trying to fine-tune the American economy in the late 1980s and early 1990s was probably misdirected. It would have been more appropriate to have criticized Congress for failing to provide a clear objective for the Federal Reserve, instead of dual targets of full employment and price stability. The lack of a clear objective probably forced Greenspan to try to fine-tune the economy in order to survive politically during the recession years of that period.

Indeed, the Federal Reserve contributes to its own problems by insisting on secrecy about what *actually* goes on in Open Market Committee meetings. The financial market often experiences short-term instability because of this secrecy and because the public is forced to guess about what the Federal Reserve is up to in its activities. By way of contrast, the world's other central banks typically hold a press conference about their actions, leaving little room for doubt and speculation. In fairness to the Federal Reserve, however, it should be noted that it too has been more forthcoming recently then in the past.

It is certainly correct that during recent years the Federal Reserve has paid little attention to monetary aggregates, concentrating instead on real variables and on financial indicators. Some economists have focused on the Federal Reserve's M2 (currency plus demand and time deposits) measure of the money supply to gauge monetary events, but this largely reflects transactions and excludes large time deposits and money market securities. Other economists view the M2 as a leading indicator of the nominal gross national product (GNP). A slump in the M2 is interpreted as a forecast of a slump in general economic activity.

Critics are quick to point out that there is little reason to believe that money figures are better guides to economic activity currently than in the past. In their view this is little more than the revival of monetarism, which fell out of favor because the various monetary indicators gave misleading readings about movements in the GNP.

The criticism is misplaced. Monetarism does not mean that changes in the money supply *automatically* cause changes in the nominal GNP. Rather, monetarists argue that while the links between changes in money and changes in economic activity are there, their lengths are anything but constant. Therefore, it is futile to try to fine-tune monetary policy by discretionary means, and it is vitally important to have a monetary rule.

Too many critics of monetarism act as though some monetary measure is the fixed point of monetarism. The fact is that one cannot so simply discuss the principal proposition of monetarism: Increases in the growth of the money supply will increase inflation in the long run and will have no lasting effect on economic activity. It is simply inappropriate to judge money's relevance by attempting to explain short-run outcomes by long-run relationships.

Evidence reported by G. P. Dwyer, Jr., and R. W. Hafer in their study of several countries is consistent with these relationships. From 1979 to 1984, the relationship between money growth and nominal income in sixty-two countries was very close. There was little systematic relationship between money growth and real income, and there was a one-for-one correlation between money growth and inflation. Moreover, for the period

1981–1986, evidence from forty countries supported the same conclusions.[10]

It seems that the Federal Reserve System under Alan Greenspan has also registered success in the closing years of the 1990s. For one, Greenspan has demonstrated that low inflation, low unemployment, and rapid growth can coexist much longer than some economists believed. In good part Greenspan's credibility as an inflation fighter has helped. He could well afford not to pay too much attention to the received economic wisdom about inflation, employment, and growth. Moreover, Greenspan appears to hold little confidence in the sophisticated and new mathematical models as guides for monetary and fiscal policies. His preference, apparently, for a more pragmatic and flexible approach to policy has yielded much applause and little criticism. In some respects he appears a worthy successor to Benjamin Strong of the Federal Reserve's early era.

NOTES

1. See George Macesich, *World Economy at the Crossroads* (Westport, Conn.: Praeger, 1997), p. 35.

2. *Report to the Congress of the Commission on the Role of Gold in the Domestic and International Monetary System*, Vols. 1 and 2. (Washington, D.C.: Secretary of the Treasury, March 1982). See also Anna J. Schwartz, "Introduction," in *A Retrospective on the Classical Gold Standard, 1821–1931*, Michael D. Bordo and Anna J. Schwartz, eds. (Chicago: University of Chicago Press, 1984), pp. 1–20.

3. Milton Friedman, "Commodity-Reserve Currency," *Journal of Political Economy* 59, June 1951: 203–232. Reprinted in Milton Friedman ed. *Essays in Positive Economics* (Chicago: University of Chicago Press, 1953), pp. 133–156.

4. See the exchange between W. Lee Hoskins, "Defending Zero Inflation: All for Naught," Federal Reserve Bank of Minneapolis, *Quarterly Review* (Spring 1991): 16–20; and S. Rao Aiyagari, "Response to a Defense of Zero Inflation," Federal Reserve Bank of Minneapolis, *Quarterly Review* (Spring 1991): 21–24.

5. For a discussion of supporting empirical evidence, see George Macesich and Hui-Liang Tsai, *Money in Economic Systems* (New York: Praeger, 1982).

6. See Milton Friedman, "The Role of Monetary Policy," *American Economic Review* 58, March 1968: 1–17.

7. See Anna J. Schwartz, "Short-Term Targets of Three Central Banks," in *Targets and Indicators of Monetary Policy*, Karl Brunner, ed. (San Francisco: Chandler, 1969).

8. See M. W. Keran, "Selecting a Monetary Indicator: Evidence from the United States and Other Developed Countries," *Review*, Federal Reserve Bank of

St. Louis (September 1970): 8–19; G. P. Dwyer, Jr., and R. W. Hafer, "Is Money Irrelevant?" *Review*, Federal Reserve Bank of St. Louis (May/June 1988): 3–17.

9.   See Macesich and Tsai, *Money in Economic Systems*, pp. 85–133.

10.   Dwyer and Hafer, "Is Money Irrelevant?"

Chapter 7

Contemporary Commercial Banking

BUSINESS OF BANKING

Contemporary commercial banks may be described as financial department stores. Although banks may provide many services to the community, their principal business is the lending and investing of money and handling deposits. This is their "stock and trade." In peddling their wares commercial banks attempt to maximize their returns in a manner similar to other profit-making concerns in the private sector of the economy.

There are two types of returns that a businessperson will consider in running his or her own or another's business concern and indeed that an individual will take into account in choosing an occupation. They are pecuniary returns and nonpecuniary returns. Pecuniary returns are the most easily understood in that they are quantifiable. The information is provided by wage rates, monies, or from the financial statements of business concerns. The latter for the most part indicate clearly the size of the monetary return that the business organization has managed to obtain from the sale of its products. Nonpecuniary returns, however, are more illusive because they are not really quantifiable.

In the case of an individual confronted with an occupational choice, for example, nonpecuniary returns depend on his or her tastes and preferences in evaluating the nonmonetary advantages or disadvantages of an occupation. A steady but modest monetary income with congenial coworkers is preferred by some people to the preferences of others for large and pecuniary incomes obtainable in more disagreeable surroundings. Similarly, a businessperson may prefer a "take things easy" attitude and so a modest monetary return for his or her organization as compared to the greater exertion that a larger pecuniary return would require. A banker may prefer this "easy life" that safety of greater liquidity offers to the pecuniary income that he or she will lose through this attitude. In fact, in the past moderate but consistent monetary returns was a characteristic of the banking industry.

In their attempts to allocate available bank funds so as to maximize monetary and nonmonetary returns bankers as businesspeople must solve the dual problems of liquidity and solvency. At the same time, these problems must be solved within limitations imposed by legal considerations. The amount of liquidity actually needed by an individual bank is of fundamental importance. Too much liquidity means that a bank is forgoing pecuniary returns and thus may not earn what is considered a "normal" return so that stockholders will permanently withdraw their funds from the bank and employ them where such a return, or a better one is obtainable. Too little liquidity, on the other hand, may be fatal to the life of a bank and perhaps disturbing to the banker's peace of mind.

As important as liquidity is to a bank as a going concern it alone cannot guarantee solvency. In this matter banks are not different from other businesses. Thus a business may be liquid enough to meet all its liabilities currently due and for which payment is demanded and still be insolvent. A business concern to be solvent must, at a minimum, possess assets whose total value is as great as the sum of its liabilities to outsiders. Finally, legal considerations impose restrictions on the monetary returns that a bank may earn by limiting its holdings of certain categories of earning assets and excluding others.

INPUT "MIX"

As distinct from other businesses, commercial banks take pride in their debt obligations to the public. This is drawn from the fact that if bankers had to depend upon their own capital there would indeed be very few banks on the contemporary scene. Deposits (demand and time) are the chief ingredients in the input "mix" of banks.[1] They are used to manufacture the industry's principal product, which is bank credit.

One source of these deposits is the public's surrender of cash to the bank. The second source is granting of loans and making investments. The former are known as primary deposits and the latter as derived deposits. Individual bankers view derived deposits as tending to reduce their cash reserves and so they encourage an increase in pecuniary deposits as a means of enabling them to increase their loan created (or investment created) derived deposits. Thus, they attempt to increase confidence in their institution by advertising their debt obligation to present depositors thereby hoping to encourage others to make deposits with them.

The type and nature of the deposit liabilities to the public and important determinants of a bank's input "mix." Commercial bank deposits in the United States may be classified broadly into demand, time, and savings deposits and subclassified according to the nature of the depositor: (1) private individuals, partnerships, corporation; (2) states and political subdivisions; (3) the U.S. government; and (4) foreign.

It is generally agreed that classification of deposits according to the function they perform does not yield clear lines of demarcation. Demand deposits are typically held for the purpose of making payments. Time and savings deposits are an investment outlet for individual savers. There is, however, considerable interchange in the uses to which the various types of accounts are put, thereby blurring the lines drawn between their functions. In addition, banks in practice seldom exercise their right to require advance notice of withdrawals from time and savings deposits by their customers.

As in many other industries, commercial banking is not ensured a steady source of supply for its principal inputs. Private individuals who own and use demand deposits for personal convenience are the most numerous class of demand depositors. A banker can depend on regular withdrawals by this class of depositor. This source supply, normally, will not cause a banker much concern. Far more important to banks in terms of dollar volume are the deposits of businesses. Since many businesses have special seasonal and cyclical characteristics, a banker must anticipate and prepare for these deposits withdrawals by adjusting his investment portfolios so as to provide the required amount of liquidity. This may reduce the output of his principal product, namely, loans.

Local, state, and national government deposits are another source of particular concern to bankers because receipts and expenditures by various levels of government are not synchronized. For instance, at certain times of the year when taxes are collected, deposits in public accounts increase substantially and decline in other times when expenditures are heavy. Since coincidence between the deposits of taxpayers and recipients of government checks cannot be counted upon by an individual bank, bankers attempt to offset the public accounts they hold by a high degree of liquidity in their assets and so reduce loan output.

The behavior of foreign deposits is perhaps the least predictable. Their behavior is influenced by a wide range of foreign and domestic factors. Bankers are not readily disposed to use these funds in other than highly liquid activities. Most of these accounts are carried by commercial banks in New York City.

Other major sources of bank funds and ingredients in a bank's input mix are its own capital, including surplus, individual profits, and reserves for losses, and funds borrowed from other banks and the Federal Reserve System.

OUTPUT "MIX"

Loans

Although investments and loans are both important "products" of commercial banks, loans are their primary form of output. A banker with a decided preference for pecuniary returns, will ceteris paribus, also prefer this type of output because of its higher pecuniary return. Loan output "mix" consists of short-term commercial loans, term loans, real estate loans, consumer loans, and security loans.

Business firms are the major customers for short-run commercial loans. Demand for this type of loan is very sensitive to economic fluctuations rising during the upswing of economic activity when business is prosperous and declining in the downswing. Coupled with its cyclical sensitivity is its seasonal variation. There is a tendency for business to increase its bank borrowing to finance the processing of the year's crop and to prepare for holiday shopping. There is also a tendency for business borrowing from banks to be directly related to inventory fluctuations. Inventory buildup or depletion will tend to be reflected in business borrowing.

Term loans are usually sought by businesses that are too small to use credit markets, or by larger firms that prefer to seek term credit from banks rather than sell their securities. Indeed, some loans that are classified as "short term" because they are renewed periodically are in fact used by borrowers to finance permanent working capital requirements so that they are in effect term loans.

Real estate loans in the form of farm and nonfarm mortgages tend to be the province of small banks. Demand for this type of loan appears to be independent of moderate movements in general economic activity. Residential construction tends to depend mainly upon family formation, population growth, and population shifts. Commercial construction, on the other hand, is more closely related to movements in general economic activity. Farm mortgages tend to be closely associated with the purchase of land, which is influenced by the movement of agricultural prices.

Consumer loans are another important element in the output mix of commercial banks. Moreover, banks also meet consumer demands for loans in an indirect manner. They finance consumers indirectly through loans to dealers in durable goods, sales finance companies, as well as other lending agencies. These loans tend to conform closely to movements in general economic activity. In addition, they appear to be affected by the willingness of consumers to increase their debt, which in turn appears to be influenced by evaluation of their past and future incomes.

Security loans are another element in a bank's loan output mix. These loans fall into broad categories: "street loans" (e.g., brokers and dealers in securities), or loans made to others for the purpose of carrying securities. This type of lending constitutes an important element in the output mix of banks located in the country's principal financial centers. For most other banks in the country, however, this type of loan is a minor element in their loan output. Demand for security loans is affected primarily by changes in stock prices, current merger requirements in stocks and general new security offerings, prevailing rates on security loans, and on speculative activity in the securities markets.

Investment Output

Investments are the other major element in a bank's output mix. In terms of banking history in the United States, investment output, as represented by substantial security holdings, is a relatively recent development. During World War I security holdings by banks increased and continued to expand into the 1920s. A brief interruption occurred during 1930–1933 but thereafter the increase proceeded at an accelerated pace. Commercial bank investments increased and reached a peak of almost $100 billion during World War II.

The investment output mix of commercial banks consists of various types of security holdings by banks. Corporate bonds, municipal securities, and government securities represent the principal holdings. Corporate bonds are relatively unimportant to banks. Increased construction of various public projects by municipalities and states following World War II has resulted in a market rise in their borrowing. The satisfactory condition of local and state finances coupled with the increased vulnerability of commercial banks, federal income taxes, and the tax exempt features of local securities has resulted in a substantial holding of such securities by a commercial bank.

Holdings of U.S. government securities are by far the most important item in commercial banking's investment output. During World War II, the amount of these securities outstanding exceeded the amount that apparently could be readily absorbed by the nonbank public. Commercial banks with the aid of the Federal Reserve System, which provided them with sufficient reserves, absorbed the balance. Although banks continue to hold government securities, their importance in bank portfolios has tended to decline since 1951 following the "accord" between the Federal Reserve System and the Treasury.

PRICING OF INPUTS AND OUTPUTS

Pricing Inputs

Deposits are the most important raw material in the production of bank loans and investments. Commercial banks pay for these raw materials either through interest on time deposits or implicitly through remission of service charges on demand or checking deposits. Bankers have attempted to attract primary deposits in still other ways that do not involve direct payment for these raw materials. Architectural design of their banking establishments in the past has attempted to convey the solidity and solemnity of a Greek temple. In the postwar period, however, such design has given way to a more up-to-date approach, giving banking establishments a modernistic flair.

Banks have engaged in savings promotion campaigns of one form or another. They have added services to the public. Additional examples of nonprice competition in banking are readily available.

To what do we owe these "forward" strides in banking? Perhaps the most important sponsor of non-price competition for the raw materials of banking has been the Banking Act of 1933. Although this act in many respects is an advancement in American monetary and banking thought, its sponsorship of non-price competition in banking leaves much to be desired. While ostensibly protecting the public against bank failures, the act had, until recently, almost frozen commercial banking into the mold of the 1930s. Under its sponsorship banks were prohibited from paying interest on demand deposits. Furthermore, limits on interest rate payments set by the Board of Governors on time deposits closed the route of escape for the banker whose preference may have been for price competition. Government intervention and enforcement was the logical outcome of earlier attempts by local clearinghouses to set "standards" that favored monopoly. It is usually agreed that a monopoly worthy of the name cannot exist for very long unless the government's police powers are marshaled for its preservation. Attempts by clearinghouses to impose on local bankers such "standards" as (1) maximum rates of interest to be paid on deposits; (2) banking hours and banking holidays; (3) provision of multiple loans to customers; and (4) uniform charges on services were doomed to failure unless backed up with something more than threats. By 1999 serious efforts were being undertaken to reform banking laws at the federal level.

Pricing Output

Loans and investments are major elements in a bank's output mix and also its principal sources of revenue. Service charges on checking accounts and fees and commissions earned for services rendered customers are minor revenue sources. The bulk of a bank's revenues are, in effect, the product of the interest rate paid by its customers and the total volume of credit that a bank makes available.

Pricing of bank output by the banking industry differs in one important respect from practices usually followed by other industries in selling their products. The latter tend to confront their customers with established prices and terms of sales thereby permitting the exercise of consumer's choice. Banking industry, however, does not present its customers with established prices and other terms of sale. Each loan is individually negotiated between borrower and banker. Since each loan is likely to differ in its various details, the banker is apparently presented with a greater opportunity to exercise price discrimination than producers of other products.

A banker will take into consideration a number of factors in quoting a loan rate to a borrower. For example, he or she will consider the financial size of the borrower or loan, the quality and type of credit, duration of loan, the nature and degree of risk, cost of administering the loan, competition among banks, the type of collateral, the borrower's average balances maintained at the bank, the importance of the account to the bank, and the character of the banker-customer relation. Perhaps the most important determinant of loan rates, however, is the availability of alternative sources of supply to the borrower. Borrowers with no alternative sources of supply for their credit needs are often at the mercy of the local bankers.

Scattered evidence seems to suggest that it is the relatively small or medium-sized business that tends to pay a higher price for the banking industry's product. This may be attributed to the fact that a given size loan usually implies given conditions of risk, costs of administration of the loan, size of balances, and general worth to the bank. The net effect of these factors is that rates charged by banks tend to vary inversely with the size of loan. Since the loan requirements of small and medium-sized businesses are relatively modest, their rates would be expected to be higher than those paid by large business enterprises. At the same time, a large business enterprise has many alternate sources of supply at its disposal. Such an opportunity is seldom available to a modest business concern.

A number of other factors appear to also be important in limiting the ability of commercial banks to service the needs of their principal customers—the small and medium-sized businesses. Some of these factors are related to the nature of commercial banking and others to the pattern of public regulation that has restricted its operation.

In the past, bank lending has been conducted on the assumption that instability will tend to characterize the American economy. Accordingly, individual bankers will not assume ordinary risks if there is danger that the economy will be subject to sharp economic fluctuations. However, selectivity of risks by banks is attributable to the fact that banks have a relatively small cushion of equity.

The short-term and unstable character of deposit liabilities forces bankers to seek assets that will enable them to meet their liabilities under all foreseeable conditions. Even though bankers have an opportunity to borrow from the Federal Reserve System in the event of deposit withdrawal, they are concerned about the composition and stability of their deposit liabilities. Tradition and concern that such borrowing could cast doubt on their credit position has made commercial banks adverse to borrowing from the Federal Reserve System, and on this score, the Federal Reserve System had done little to allay their fears.

Laws and administrative regulation are also factors limiting risk taking on the part of banks. Banks were not permitted to underwrite security issues either directly or indirectly due to the unfortunate outcome of such practices in the 1920s and 1930s. They may not, however, hold obligations of any one obligor in amounts exceeding 10 percent of a bank's capital and surplus account. Moreover, examination of bank loan portfolios by government examiners has affected the readiness of commercial banks to make innovations in their business lending policies. Usury laws have resulted in reluctance on the part of bankers to lend money at rates in excess of "standard" or "conventional" bank rates. One consequence is that some banks turn customers away rather than change "excessive" rates, while others evade the law by employing service charges and other means to raise the gross interest rate.

UNIQUENESS OF THE BANKING INDUSTRY

Unlike other industries, the banking industry can create a multiple expansion of deposits. In a simple model of multiple deposit creation each bank can make loans up to the amount of its excess reserves, thereby creating an equal amount of deposits. The banking industry can create a multiple expansion of deposits because as each bank makes a loan and creates deposits, the reserves find their way to another bank, which uses them to make loans and create additional deposits. Given a simple model of multiple deposit creation in which banks do not hold on to excess reserves, the multiple increase in deposits equals the reciprocal of the required reserve ratio.

A more realistic model of multiple deposit creation takes into account decisions of depositors to increase their holdings of currency or of banks to hold excess reserves. As a result, there will be a smaller expansion of deposits than in the simple model. In fact, the Federal Reserve System, banks, depositors, and borrowers from banks are all important in determining the money supply. The behavior and interaction of these four actors are important building blocks in the construction of a realistic model, as discussed in Chapter 2.

Milton Friedman suggested that required reserves be set equal to 100 percent of deposits.[2] This reform is an important component of his suggested reforms of discount operations, reserve requirements, and the conduct of monetary policy so as to improve monetary control. With 100 percent reserve requirements, the money supply could be fairly in control of the Federal Reserve System because it would be equal to the monetary base. One difficulty with 100 percent reserve proposal is that it may encourage other financial institutions not subject to reserve requirements to develop substitutes that may be more like checkable deposits so as to attract funds. In this instance the Federal Reserve System may not be able to control such developments, which may well have a significant impact on the money supply.

OTHER FINANCIAL INTERMEDIARIES

In sum, banks like other financial intermediaries possess the distinguishing characteristics that they acquire funds by issuing liabilities. They in turn use the funds to acquire assets by purchasing securities or making loans. This distinguishing characteristic underscores the differences between the banking industry and other industries. Given a fractional reserve system and excess reserves, the banking industry (or system) can create a multiple expansion of deposits, ceteris paribus.

In addition to commercial banks other financial intermediaries include savings and loan associations, mutual savings banks, credit unions, and money market funds. To these may be added contractual savings institutions such as life insurance companies, pension funds, and fire and casualty insurance companies, and investment intermediaries (e.g., mutual funds, money market mutual funds, and finance companies).

Again, as in our discussion of central banking, there are important differences between American and foreign banking and other financial intermediaries. Consider the banking structure in other industrial economies. In Great Britain, France, Germany, Switzerland, Japan, Italy, Sweden, and others there are fewer dominant banks. There are usually only three or four large national banks in each country. Some banks, as in France and Italy, are state owned. Foreign banks are regularly permitted to hold shares in industrial firms. Often banks abroad can perform stock brokerage as well as banking and "merchant banking" functions. Such direct connections tend to put bankers in direct control over company policies and executive selection.

NOTES

1. This chapter adopts David Alhadeff's terminology and refers to deposits as the input of banks and loans and investments as their principal outputs. Such terminology is more accurately descriptive of the similarities among banks and other business enterprises in the private sector of the economy. See David A. Alhadeff, *Monopoly and Competition in Banking* (Berkeley: University of Califor-

nia Press, 1954). See also George Macesich, *Commercial Banking and Regional Development in the United States, 1950–1960* (Tallahassee: Florida State University Press, 1965).

2. See Milton Friedman, *A Program for Monetary Stability* (New York: Fordham University Press, 1960). See also Henry Simms, *Economic Policy for a Free Society* (Chicago: University of Chicago Press, 1948).

Chapter 8

Changing Anatomy
of Banking

CHANGING NATURE OF BANK LIABILITY MANAGEMENT

The behavior and activities of banks, especially large banks, has changed fundamentally since the 1960s. They no longer accept deposits passively. Indeed through liability management they attempt to determine their own size. Since the 1960s they issue negotiable certificates of deposit (CDs), buy federal funds, issue foreign denominated liabilities, and issue subordinated debt. Their holding companies sell commercial paper and floating rate notes, and issue long-term debt. The proceeds from their various ventures are invested in a wide and complex array of activities, from domestic loans and investments to large foreign loans. U.S. banks are interlocked with one other and with foreign banks through joint ventures and consortia. There thus seems to be no limit to the new markets and activities that U.S. banks will enter either directly or indirectly. The influence and power of banks, especially the large banks of the world, appear to give them an advantage and a seemingly endless variety of activities.

The rising aggressiveness of banks since the 1960s is consistent with the principle that competition is the best way to activate efficiency. Not everyone, however, agrees. They argue that banks' enterprising behavior makes the banking and financial system less secure, and monetary policy less effective, than if banks were more conservative in their behavior. The world debt fiasco of the 1980s, they note, is but one illustration of banks' rising aggressiveness.

It may be that the memories of loan losses and bank failures of the 1920s have now faded. It may be also that government monetary and fiscal policies since World War II have encouraged bankers to view another depression as unlikely. In either case, bankers view of government securities and other conservative financial instruments has changed. At the same time as the pace of world economic activity accelerated and was reinforced by huge petro-dollars, so did the volume of domestic and foreign requests for bank loans. Most bankers chose to accommodate their customers' loan demands. They accepted reduced liquidity in exchange for higher profits.

They had an ample store of liquidity. In 1946 American banks' cash assets and U.S. government securities accounted for almost three-quarters of their assets. By the end of the 1950s, however, bank lending capacity had largely been depleted. Although deposits had grown about 50 percent in the decade or so after the war, total bank loan volume had tripled. The loan-liquidity gap increased in the 1960s when corporations began to trim their demand deposits. Corporations no longer wished to hold large sums in interest-free checking deposits when they could use these excess funds to purchase interest-bearing Treasury bills and commercial paper.

Propelled by further loan growth and a growing shortage of funds, banks went after new sources of liquidity. The large money center banks in New York and elsewhere began issuing negotiable CDs at competitive interest rates. For all practical purposes these CDs were time deposits and carried fixed maturity dates. The practice was encouraged by the development of a secondary market for CDs which in effect meant that these instruments could be sold before maturity if an investor needed his or her funds.

As a financial innovation the CD development was particularly successful. Banks learned that liquidity could be found on both sides of the balance sheet. Thus encouraged, banks could go to the money market either with their assets or liabilities for sale. This practice of issuing liabilities at competitive rates to fulfill cash needs is called "liability management." It is possible to combine asset liquidity with liability liquidity to support further loan growth.

In addition to the CD innovation, banks in the 1960s and 1970s began issuing other manageable liabilities. Federal funds trading, which had previously occurred in limited volume, grew rapidly. Banks borrowed eurodollars from their foreign branches, and bank holding companies sold commercial paper and loaned the proceeds to their bank subsidiaries. The net effect has been that while almost none of the funds at large banks were derived from liability management in 1960 more than a third of such funds originated with such sources in 1983.[1] It is the increasing reliance on liability management as a source of bank liquidity that is raising public concern.

Liability management, nonetheless, will continue and is very likely to increase as a result of the growing competitive environment of the banking industry. In comparison to regular deposit banking, liability management is a more aggressive way to run a bank. As a result, banks are more vulnerable to shifts in the financial and money markets. Since the practice is profitable for banks, they will continue it unless otherwise directed by markets or regulatory agencies.

Factors contributing to financial innovation are important in changing the anatomy of banking and indeed the financial community in general. Most of these innovations can be attributed to economic incentives. High nominal interest rates generated by inflation and regulatory constraint have provided the necessary incentives to encourage financial innovations. In general, banks and other financial institutions use financial innovations to reduce the constraints imposed upon them by regulatory agencies as well as economic forces.

Just as technological innovations improve economic welfare, so too do financial innovations. They improve the ability of banks and other financial institutions to bear risk, lower transaction costs, and circumvent burdensome and outdated regulatory practices. They strengthen the ability of banks to serve the cluster roles they play in our theory of cooperation.[2]

NEW COMPETITIVE ENVIRONMENT

There is a feeling, some of it based on evidence, that not all banks can adjust to the new and highly competitive world of unregulated interest on deposits. Indeed in 1982 more than forty-two bank failures were registered in the United States. Expectations were confirmed that the list of troubled banks grew in the 1980s. Regulators and Congress were and indeed are showing a growing concern over these trends.

The net effect of the ongoing shake-up in American banking nevertheless promises to have a major effect on the way financial services are delivered. In the 1960s a small number of money-center banks and large insurance companies pretty much determined who got access to U.S.

financial capital. The turning point was 1974 when interest rates spiked, the stock market fell 45 percent, and large financial institutions, faced with their own problems, stopped lending to all but the highest-rated borrowers. Thousands of below-investment-grade debt instruments—including those of municipal governments and utilities—were then designated as "junk securities" because their issuers were supposedly on the verge of bankruptcy. When the issuers survived investors realized very handsome profits.

The lesson was not lost on many Wall Street firms. By 1977 they were issuing high-yield securities for a broad range of below-investment-grade companies. Although considered "high risk" these securities turned out to carry less portfolio risk than higher-rated instruments because yield premiums were then compensated for defaults. Leaders of small- and medium-sized firms with good prospects, who had been dependent on relationships with individual banks and insurance companies, could now turn to a market-based system with thousands of institutional buyers, including the rapidly growing mutual funds that eventually became larger than many banks.

For their part banks moved aggressively into new lines of business and geographical regions even as competition for businesses outside the traditional banking community increased. Thus in March 1983, Citicorp, the second-largest bank holding company in the United States at the time, broke the barrier between big U.S. commercial banks and the business of selling insurance when it agreed, in principle, to buy the American State Bank in Rapid City, South Dakota. A month later the First Interstate Bankcorp followed suit by buying Big Stone State Bank in Big Stone, South Dakota. Security Pacific Bankcorp, too, announced its intention to open a subsidiary in South Dakota where it expected to sell insurance. All of this came about in March 1983 when South Dakota allowed bank holding companies to circumvent federal regulations by purchasing or establishing a state chartered subsidiary through which they could sell insurance. U.S. Congress in October 1982 had tried to restrict the insurance operation that a bank can have, but it left a loophole by omitting any reference to state-chartered subsidiaries, and that paved the way for the South Dakota law the banks had been seeking. Other states soon followed.

Many observers believe that the banks' large customer bases and branch networks will enable them to offer a variety of insurance products at very competitive prices because of high volume and low start-up costs. That would be a boon to consumers but it would also force insurers to reduce shrinking profit margins on such important insurance products as whole life and property/casualty insurance.

Banks have also entered the brokerage business to establish a beachhead from which to move into other more profitable securities operations like underwriting and distributing new stock issues for corporations. At the same time, banks moved into other areas of financial services.

This change in the pattern of banking activity, moreover, has taken place without radical revisions in the two key American banking laws. Thus the Glass-Steagall Act of 1933 separated the banking and brokerage business. Brokerage houses could not take deposits and banks could not buy and sell stocks for customers. Until relatively recently they were minor players in the securities industry.

Congress continues, at this writing, to debate the country's bank regulatory system. The system worked well enough until the roaring inflation of the 1970s made investors more interest rate conscious. The birth of money-market mutual funds set off a fierce savings war between Main Street banks and Wall Street investment houses.

Driving the trend, as well, has been an explosion in the use of computers and other electronic systems including electronic funds transfer systems. The effect has been to lower transactions costs in ways simply unforeseen by the legislation of the 1930s. Computers also can keep track of all of the customer's needs, opening vast potential markets for firms. For instance, an automatic teller machine could be used to place a stock order as well as to check a savings balance.

Despite such incentives, critics worry that the marketplace is getting too risky. Some question whether money-management conglomerates have the talent needed to successfully manage their diversified organizations. Others argue that mixing banking with general commerce could pose an even bigger threat. For instance, there is no sure way to insulate a conglomerate's banking subsidiary from economic difficulties experienced by nonbanking units.

On the other hand, much of the opposition to changes in banking laws comes from people anxious to protect their own piece of the business. Several banks object to the economic power big banks can wield if allowed to move across state lines or merge with multinational industrial corporations. Their fear is that such firms could have undue influence on legislators and even foreign governments.

There is little doubt that, stripped of pervasive regulator support, the banking system in the years ahead will consolidate markedly in response to the demand and supply of financial services. Indeed, forecasts are for thousands rather than hundreds of bank and other financial service mergers in the near term. Some of the forecasts suggest that much of the activity will take place at middle-tier banks. Small one-branch community banks will likely survive, due to their very strong relationships in the local markets. These markets are not large enough to attract major competitors. Large money-center banks are likely to remain strong competitors due to economies of scale that they can bring in lowering their costs of providing financial services.

It is, however, the middle-sized banks (those with assets of several hundred million dollars to several billion dollars) who will decide whether to be predators or prey. These banks typically have relatively high cost structures, and fifty or more branches. They are not entrenched in their markets as small banks are in theirs and the markets where medium-sized banks operate are large enough to attract major competitors. Markets may also become more segmented—whereby some banks will deal almost exclusively with the affluent customers, some will become more efficient business banks and some will find efficient ways to serve the ordinary customer.

The concern with which bank regulators view the newfound freedom of banks is suggested by the moves at the federal level to put more discipline on the financial conglomerates. At the same time the F.D.I.C. and other federal-insurance agencies propose a major revision of deposit-insurance rules to make bank managers, shareholders, and big depositors assume some of the costs if a bank fails.

The system in place at the time of this writing provides that federal agencies bear most of the costs when a bank fails. Under the F.D.I.C. plan, savers with no more than $100,000 would be fully protected, while people with larger deposits would not have full protection. Other measures aimed at slowing down the financial revolution were also put in place on the federal level.

Few people believe that such measures would more than slow the financial revolution. It is more likely that formal regulation will be supplemented with market discipline. In effect, investors and depositors will be provided with better information about financial institutions. Banks will be required, for instance, to disclose more about past-due loans, interest-rate sensitivities, and deposit maturity structures.

Another F.D.I.C. proposal would let state-chartered banks that it insures underwrite corporate securities. This is an important departure from the post-depression era separation of the investment-banking industries. To be sure, the F.D.I.C. proposal includes sound recommendations to insulate banks from the financial risks that might result from underwriting.

Under the proposal, banks could engage in underwriting only through subsidiaries. The subsidiaries would have to be physically separate from their affiliated banks and they cannot use the banks' names. It would also require three fairly conservative approaches to underwriting. One option would be to underwrite securities only on a *best effort basis*—meaning the banks would try their best to sell the securities they underwrite but would not be required to purchase any unsold securities. Alternately, banks could choose to confine their underwriting to highly rated securities, or banks could limit their underwriting to shares in mutual funds that invest in short-term liquid assets.

The proposal would also limit the amount banks could lend both to companies whose securities they underwrite and to customers buying such securities. The restrictions are designed to prevent banks from taking loan risks to support their underwriting activities. Concerns about such potential conflicts of interest between underwriting and lending were a major reason for laws separating commercial and investment banking.

The Federal Reserve is strongly opposed to letting banks underwrite corporate securities, but if the F.D.I.C.'s interpretation of the law contained in its proposal is correct, the Fed would be powerless to prevent state-chartered banks, or non-Fed member banks from getting into the business.

If the F.D.I.C. puts its plan into effect, national banks and other banks belonging to the Federal Reserve System might be tempted to switch charters so as to get into the underwriting business. If that happens it would be an uncanny repeat of history.

In the years leading up to the 1920s, federal law prevented national banks from underwriting corporate securities. But many states did not impose such restrictions. In the 1920s many banks began switching to state charters to get into the securities business. To stem the decline in the number of national banks, the federal government dropped its restrictions in 1927. They were reimposed in 1933 after it was learned that some banks had run into trouble partly because of free-wheeling dealings of their securities affiliates. By then, the 1929 stock market crash had damaged banks' enthusiasm for securities activities.

The vision of banking implicit in the current regulatory position is indeed broad. It includes the traditional banking services including commercial lending plus insurance, securities, real estate, and savings and loan associations. In essence banks are now viewed as financial service enterprises though still separate from activities generally considered as commercial, for example, manufacturing or retail sales.

The regulatory situation for the authorities will very likely become even more complex. Consider, for instance, the spread of the Internet. It is reported that Bank One Corp in June 1999 has established a new business unit to sell a range of financial services over the Internet.[3] Evidently, the aim is to expand the nation's fourth-largest bank through the Internet rather than by acquisitions. While Bank One already sells services on the Internet, the new business unit called Wingspan establishes a district, nationwide Web presence, taking the company beyond the fourteen midwestern and southwestern states where it has branches.

According to reports the move by Bank One is one of the most aggressive thus far by a major bank to pursue new customers over the Internet. Other big banks have offered online banking mainly as an additional service for existing customers. This approach is very similar to that of such discount brokerage firms as Charles Schwab Corp., which uses the Internet as a primary marketing avenue for a variety of financial offerings. The bank's entry will almost certainly add competitive pressure on fledgling Internet-only banks lacking the resources and product range of a large diversified bank with $250 billion in assets in 1999.

Bank One's new unit Wingspan is to repackage for the Interest services previously sold through branches, a separate Bank One Web site and the direct marketing machinery of the company's First USA credit card operation. The service amounts to a separate distribution channel for the bank's checking accounts, certificate of deposits, credit cards, mortgages, insurance mutual funds, electronic bill payment, and stock brokerage. Wingspan's customers are also to have free access to Bank One automated teller machines. In addition, the bank will reimburse these customers for up to four ATM fees a month incurred at machines outside the Bank One network.

The increased competitive environment will almost certainly strengthen the banking and financial role in the domestic as well as international economy. This can only be encouraged.

BANKERS AND THEIR CLIENTS: COUNTRY PRACTICE

In search for solutions to their financial problems, banks and their clients often fear that other countries are doing better, and indeed in some instances this is true. Though the various approaches and practices are not necessarily transferable, their study can be constructive. Given that the world's money and financial markets are highly interdependent, various approaches and practices, however unique to a given country, spill over and influence other countries.

In Canada, for instance, the relationship between banker and client is very close indeed. At times such a relationship presents a serious problem to bank and client. Consider the case of the Canadian Imperial Bank of Commerce (CIBC). It is one of Canada's largest banks and one that prides itself most on being banker to Canadian big business. In Canada to be a main bank to a company is considered very important. It means that there are no rules restricting lending to any one customer to a certain percentage of capital. Unlike banks elsewhere it is thus not forced to parcel out or syndicate big loans among competitors. As a result, a company's main bank is very much involved with the company. A case in point was reported in *The Economist*.[4] When a series of setbacks in 1978 overtook Massey-Ferguson, the world's largest producer of tractors and second-largest producer of combine harvesters as well as CIBC's client, the bank was left with a large bad debt. It left CIBC also with a desire to spread the risk of large corporate clients more widely and a determination to monitor more closely its customers in the corporate sector.

Indeed, it is the need to monitor corporate clients that has been underscored by the experience of banks. In most economies failure to monitor properly or even publish (let alone analyze) data on a corporation's or company's financial health has had disastrous consequences. Chronic financial mismanagement has gone unnoticed.

The fast pace of inflation during the decades of the 1960s and 1970s has led firms to rely increasingly on shorter-term borrowing, and average maturity of the debt has decreased sharply. At the same time, firms have sold off their short-term financial assets so that their liquidity ratios, that is, financial assets divided by short-term liabilities, have also worsened during these years. These ratios appear to fluctuate with the business cycle deteriorating at the outset of the cycle and improving toward the end.

The tendency over recent cycles, however, has been that these ratios are not being restored to the precycle values. There appears a general deterioration in the values over the several post-war cycles. Their restoration, according to some observers, requires massive corporate bank and equity issues. For instance, in the early 1950s American corporations' short-term debt was a little more than a third of long-term debt. In 1982 it was almost 100 percent. Furthermore, the long-term debt of twenty- to thirty-year bonds is increasingly replaced by five- to ten-year loans and rates. For the same years, the ratios of American corporations' liquid assets to their short-term market debt has fallen to less than half.

According to the New York firm of Solomon Brothers, whose 1982 report on the financial deterioration of American corporations makes a case for such deterioration, inflation and increased borrowings are good for business. That is to say, by borrowing to finance acquisitions of real producing assets whose value appreciates while the liability depreciates is simply not correct. It is not good for business as is often implied. The report underscores that in 1949 the up-to-date valuation of net worth of American nonfinancial business was $2.02 for each dollar of debt. By the end of the 1970s the ratio was $1.36. In short, as inflation and borrowing have accelerated, equity prices have lagged. The supposed higher return to shareholders has not materialized for the same reason that the value that the market has put on each increment of current-cost net worth brought about by new borrowing has not occurred as rapidly.

A similar situation also appears to exist in other countries during these years. Drawing on the June 1982 quarterly report of the Bank of England, *The Economist* observes that average debt-equity ratios for British industrial and commercial companies were at a sixteen-year low in 1981. To judge from another unpublished study by the Bank of England, the experience of British companies mirrors that of the American. One important difference is that the real return on capital employed dropped further and faster between the early 1960s and 1981, when it hit a low of 3 percent in Britain, than in any major industrial country.

Italy with accelerating inflation and higher debt-equity ratios than in Britain had significantly increased debt-servicing costs. In a 1981 study by Mediobanca, which is the country's long-term lender, high interest ratios are reported as responsible for restricting many of the country's companies from undertaking long-overdue modernization and expansion programs. The results of the study indicate that in private-sector companies about 70 percent of the preinterest profits go to interest changes.

For this period in France available corporate data are sketchy. Such scattered evidence as exists suggests that French companies' need for external financing is considerably greater than in Britain, Germany, or the United States. Internal funds as a proportion of spending are fixed assets and stocks were only 51 percent in France in 1981 compared with 80 percent in Germany, 88 percent in the United States, and 108 percent in Britain.

In Germany concern with long-term deterioration in the industrial capital base is underscored by a Bundesbank report in November 1982 citing a modest rise in companies equity (or own funds) of only 3 percent. Thus in 1981, equity accounted for only 20.5 percent of the balance sheet total compared with 21 percent in 1980, 26.5 percent in 1970, and roughly 30 percent in 1965.

The Bundesbank is aware of the reasons for the decline—including at the top of its list—the insufficient earning power of the enterprises. This in turn has prevented firms from generating adequate internal funds. Potential investors are hesitant to provide risk capital. Firms, as a result, were pushed to resort to increase borrowing leading to additional interest payments and thus to a further reduction in earnings.

By Japanese standards the country's firms during these years appear to be doing well in terms of financing. Thus the Bank of Japan reports that the corporate sector's demand for external finance has dropped. In 1974 it was 11.3 percent of gross domestic product. On the other hand, OECD (Organization for Economic Cooperation and Development) estimates for July 1982 show the ratio of liquid assets to current liabilities slipping to 0.28 in 1980 and 1981. This would appear to be about the same as for the United States. These figures, however, are not strictly comparable.

Nevertheless, the estimates do suggest that for the period and the countries under review there is a pronounced deterioration in the corporate sector of the economy. To judge from the estimates quoted in the Solomon firm study, more than $10 billion a month in 1983 in the United States would have been required to restore the corporate debt-maturity ratios even to the levels of the early 1970s. According to *The Economist* study cited earlier, the monthly average in 1983 is estimated to be about $3 billion, significantly below the figures reported as required by the Solomon firm if the American corporate sector is to reverse its secular decline.

The deterioration of the industrial capital base in many countries during these years prompted banks to evaluate their relationship with money of their best customers. To judge from evidence reported by the top twenty American regional banks for 1982 they were discounting 0.73 percent of their average loans outstanding of earnings on the assumption that they would not be repaid. This is worse than the 0.56 percent reached in 1976. These are for domestic customers and do not include the more dubious foreign loans.

The changing relationship between banks and their corporate customers is also suggested by the prevalence in America of disintermediation or short-cutting the banking system. Thus, corporations no longer turn to banks for short-term credit. They now issue commercial paper that is picked up by the money market funds. The amount of such paper in the United States doubled between the end of 1979 and the middle of 1982.

Likewise, the decreased credit rating of many corporations has also pushed their paper out of the money market funds and back to bank borrowing. At the same time banks offer to back up lines of credit to many companies in the event that their access to the market is closed. In any case, the changing relationship reinforced by borrowers shifting to commercial paper forced banks to look elsewhere. Flush with OEPC deposits in the 1970s, banks were forced to do something with these deposits if returns were to be earned. Some found an outlet for profitable loans in corporations too small to issue their own commercial paper. This was indeed lucrative for banks so engaged since they could charge at prime rate or above to these firms without worry that their loan offers would be turned down. This is the development of the so-called *middle market* in the United States facilitated by the increasing scope of nationwide banking.

Competition in the middle market, however, has reduced banking profits due to the entry of many more banks into the market. In addition, the smaller corporations themselves began to understand better their own improved bargaining position, which resulted in many receiving loans at the prime rate or even below.

As a result of the growing indebtedness of American corporations the role of bank lending has also changed. In many corporations it is now increasingly long-term rather than short-term cyclical finance provided by commercial paper. Indeed, banks are being tied more closely to their corporate customers as a result. Banks now find it difficult to lose one of their clients however desirable that may be for the bank. Nonetheless, banks have also learned as a result that they must be actively involved in a corporate crisis if they are to influence the outcome.

In financially sophisticated Britain critics charge that banks have not invested enough in industry. What they did lend was short term and not enough. Banks claim that while they are prepared to lend for a longer period, they can not force on their clients fixed-term loans. Industry has apparently a preference for the flexibility of an overdraft, which is typically used in Britain.

Moreover, British banks do not wish to become major equity holders in the business of their clients. In fact, it is because they avoided becoming shareholders, so the argument goes, that British banking is characterized by stability that it presumably would not otherwise have. There are, however, some notable exceptions where banks have stepped in and converted loans into preference shares. British banks do support their clients, sometimes with the assistance of the Bank of England. this is usually the case where several banks are involved in a troubled company. The Bank of England assumes a coordinating role for the banks' efforts at rescue.

Indeed, the Bank of England, unlike most central banks, has always been just a bank and manages to keep a hand, so to speak, in a few commercial accounts so as to keep in touch with the world outside central banking. Its involvement as coordinator in industrial rescue operations, however, goes beyond this. It has always acted as sort of a semi-official go-between. Unlike in the United States rescue operations are not guided by banks, nor by the central government as in France and Germany, nor by law as in Italy, but rather by the Bank of England.

This role for the Bank of England is explained by the absence in British companies of any one lead bank as in Germany and France and many small banks as in the United States. The cooperation and coordination is thus made simpler between the Bank of England and the big London clearing banks. Observers have remarked that it would indeed be ironic if the British system of coordination and reserve operations would lead to more industrial rescues and for longer. After all, the Bank of England is also the supervisor of banks and responsible for ensuring that they are not reckless in their operation.

The German universal system of banking maintains a durable and interlocking relationship with the country's industries. This arrangement has been suggested by many observers in the past as a model for other countries. Not even Germany and its universal banking system has been spared dealing with serious problems of the 1970s and 1980s. The German banking system is in fact more deeply committed and involved with whatever industrial rescue operations may be required than is true of banks in other countries. There is, moreover, little they can expect in the way of support from the government.

Such an arrangement has permitted German banks to swap debt for equity during the 1930s while in the United States the Glass-Steagall Act prohibits such activities. This is but an illustration of the considerable power exercised by German banks. This has led, in turn, to conflicts of interest on more than one occasion. Some banks, for instance, have become entangled with the affairs of their clients that they may be at the same time its client's biggest creditor and principal shareholder.

Various German commissions, however, viewed the possibility of conflict of interest as not a significant problem with universal banking. Thus the Gessler Commission in the late 1970s recommended that banks should merely draw up a code of good conduct. A more restrictive recommendation was that banks should be limited to 25 percent plus one share in their holdings of industrial equities. There is, moreover, a problem of selling off the large pieces of industrial equities that banks hold without disrupting the economy. Owing to its limitations, the German stock market provides little help in this direction.

One reason for the relative underdevelopment of the German stock market may well be that bankers make a better profit by lending than by issuing stocks and bonds. This is also suggested by the capital base of German industry in terms of the decline of its own funds in total balance from 27 percent to 20 percent over the decade of the 1970s and 1980s. Indeed there has not been a major bond issue in Germany during the entire decade of the 1970s. How long German banks will be able to support financially such troublesome heavy industry giants as well continues to be an open question.

It is said that in France wherever money moves, the bank of the centralist government can be found directing it. This is understandable. The country's three largest commercial banks have been nationalized since 1946. Neither right-wing nor socialist governments in France see any reason why they should not be nationalized and with the arrival of the socialists in 1981 the remaining banks, except the 150 or so foreign banks, were nationalized. Thus, the idea of government intervention into the country's economy is not a monopoly of any single political party.

Big French companies have a so-called *lead bank*, which is the company's biggest creditor. It is one of the responsibilities of the lead bank to file with the French central bank every one of the company's credit facilities over $3.7 million (Fr. 25 million in 1983). The lead bank is, in effect, also in charge of the six to twelve banks that typically constitute a company's principal creditors.

If problems develop with one of its clients, the lead bank takes up the case with CIRI (the Comité Interministériel de Reconstruction de l'Industrie), which in effect is charged with dealing with the country's financially sick companies. The organization is as mysterious and forbidding as the Paris Club, which is an informal group of Western government creditors, to the heavily indebted developing countries. Some indeed have described it as a "black box." It is composed of representatives from several French ministries and a secretariat whose members search out and discuss a company's problems with bankers, unions, and suppliers to determine a course of action to be recommended to the CIRI and by it to the government.

There are a number of obvious problems connected with CIRI. For instance, what does it do when confronted with a sick private company that is in competition with a nationalized one? What does CIRI do when domestic buyers for a company cannot be found but it is reluctant to sell to a foreigner? What role do foreign banks have in the bailouts? Can government really make decisions on only economic and not social grounds? Since bankers and industrialists in the country take orders from ministries and not the market, can CIRI be sure that all wisdom lies within the ministries?

Italian industry's dependence on banks is well known. So too is the large number of banks (1,080 in 1982) serving the country's industries. A medium-sized company commonly deals with twenty to thirty banks, a big one with forty to fifty. The country's system of credit ceilings, which are the government's only control over the money supply, also encourages a company in dealing with many banks. Thus, if any one bank is close to its credit ceiling the company can readily turn to another.

In effect, Italian companies are heavily dependent on short-term rates. They cannot readily move into a longer-term market since loans lasting over eighteen months are in the hands of special long-term lending institutions that must issue bonds in competition with the government and its significant deficit (amounting to almost 17 percent of the GDP in 1982). When an Italian company is in trouble there is no lead bank or house bank to which it can turn. It turns to the laws for help. For such help it can call on three important laws passed during the difficult financial period of the 1970s. Thus LAW 675 is the government's safety net and the only restructuring law that allows direct contributions from the state. LAW 787 was designed specifically to restructure the country's troubled chemical industry. LAW 95 is most widely used and permits a court judgment to freeze a troubled company's debts for two to three years with a moratorium on interest-rate payments. New loans can be authorized by court decree and thus be made eligible for government guarantees. Indeed, it is expected that these laws may be extended to include so-called healthy companies if it can be shown that financial restructuring would help them to be more competitive internationally.

Elsewhere on the continent significant differences also exist. In particular former Yugoslavia prior to its disastrous breakup in the 1990s provides a unique combination of socialist and market elements in its banking organization that may well have more than historical interest. It merits a closer examination.[5]

"Basic banks" represented the case of former Yugoslavia's banking system. They performed the main part of financial intermediation. They were "mixed" banks, engaged in all bank operations: short term and long term; domestic and foreign; with socialist and private subjects. They were primarily funded by Organizations of Associated Labor (or OALs) by self-management agreement and represented their "associations" in performing services in financing.

An important consequence of such management is that basic banks are not profit-oriented institutions. They are primarily designed to provide for their members the maximum of financial resources at the minimum cost. In addition to OALs' members, basic banks may be internal banks of OALs (similar to the finance department of companies), self-management communities, and other socialist institutions, excluding governments.

Organization of basic banks differs in important respects from profit-motivated banks elsewhere. Thus the top management body of the bank is the assembly, comprising representatives of all members of the bank with equal voting power. The assembly elects the executive board responsible for the implementation of its decisions and guidelines. It also appoints the manager of the bank responsible for the efficient working of the bank and implementations of decisions taken by the assembly and by the executive board. The assembly also elects credit committees that decide on individual credit applications, within the framework of credit policy designed by the assembly and executive board. Finally, the supervision board, elected by the assembly, is responsible for the legal conformity of bank operations. The bank's staff has its own management bodies, responsible for decision making on employment and dismissal of personnel, incomes (within the framework decided by the assembly), and working conditions. The highest management body is the assembly of workers' community, which elects the workers' council and committees responsible for the various activities. These workers' management bodies, however, do not decide on bank policies.

Although banks are not profit oriented, there is a net income. These banks usually have three funds: reserve fund, joint liability fund, and business fund. The reserve fund is designed for securing bank liquidity. Therefore, resources of this fund are held on account with the central banking system. The joint liability fund is aimed at covering losses resulting from uncollectable claims. The business fund provides for resources for fixed assets of the bank (premises, equipment, and so on). In addition to these funds, bank solvency is guaranteed by its members by their total assets (unlimited guarantee). In addition to these mandatory funds, banks my have other funds as decided by the assembly.

Basic banks represent financial institutions that are, on the one hand, very similar to banks in developed market economies and on the other hand also rather different from these banks. They are similar in their operations to banks in developed market economies; they are different in respect to their motive. They are not profit oriented; their operations are primarily motivated by the needs for financing on the part of their members who are at the same time their main borrowers. This results in motivation for maximizing the amount of credit availability and minimizing the cost of credit at the same time. Also, their operations are significantly determined by their share in financing of priority needs listed in social plans, and accepted by banks by signing self-management agreements.

Next in importance in the former Yugoslavia's unique financial structure are associated banks. They are established only by basic banks. Legislation permitted considerable freedom for banks to transfer various types of their operations to these associated banks, or to use them as their agents for all types of domestic and foreign transactions, excluding sight deposits and operations with individuals. In practice foreign exchange operations were the main operations of these banks. In this way, associated banks represented institutions that significantly contributed to the integration of the banking system, though mainly within the individual former six republics.

Both basic banks and associated banks were obligated to implement monetary measures decided on by the central banking system. The central banking system supervised bank liquidity and prescribed measures for improvement of the liquidity of individual banks. It decided on penalties if these measures were not followed and initiated the judiciary procedure against such banks and their management.

Basic and associated banks were allowed to perform foreign transactions only if they fulfilled a list of conditions ensuring that the bank was able to perform these operations successfully. In case a bank failed to settle its foreign obligations by the date of maturity, the National Bank of Yugoslavia (i.e., the central bank) may settle the obligation and then order the Social Accounting Service (which handled the giro account of the bank) to charge its account for the dinar counterpart of the obligation paid on behalf of the bank, in favor of the National Bank of Yugoslavia.

To American and European observers Japanese industrial finance is too debt-heavy and bank dependent. This may have been adequate during a time when banks and industries had a unity of purpose. This may no longer be true as indeed events in the 1990s demonstrated. Most Japanese companies have a main bank similar to the lead bank in France and the house bank in Germany. The importance of the main bank to a company depends on which of the three predominant corporate structures it belongs to. In the facility controlled Zaibatsus, for example, Mitsubishi, Sumimoto, and similar groups along with manufacturing, trading, and other companies can be found banking at a commercial bank. The banks are simply part of the entity without a dominant influence on the group's activities.

In groups such as Sanwa and Dai-Ichi Kangyo the bank tends to be more dominant and the interlinking of the group's companies tend to be the weakest. The units are more independent financially than in the traditional Zaibatsus.

The third group focuses around such manufacturing entities as Toyota. The group's trading company acts as a banker to the large number of small suppliers in such groups. Ties with any given commercial bank are not as close.

The Japanese system is, in effect, geared to commercial decision making so that bankers do not play as important a role as in Germany. There are no proxy votes and little actual power is in the hands of bankers. The power structure is tilted to the production rather than the financial or banking side of business. This does not mean that Japanese bankers are without power. They do have power and they exercise it. Although commercial and investment banking is legally separated as in the United States, securities firms have charged that interference by bankers in industry's affairs has been a key reason why companies have tried to reduce their dependence on bank finance. Indeed, through the 1980s and into the 1990s big Japanese companies moved into the open market as a source of external funds.

Resorting to the capital markets for external financing by Japanese companies, however, is far from easy. Only the largest and best companies can pass the severe tests imposed on entry into these markets. It is charged, moreover, that banks are strongly opposed to any loosening of these requirements, which would permit more entries into the market. Banks have good reason to resist changes since the share of bank borrowings in the total of small- and medium-sized companies has remained fairly steady.

In times of troubles, however, a company can turn to its lead or main bank for more than solace and advice. It can count on its bank to act as a rallying point or catalyst for a solution. There is seldom talk of receivership or liquidations. Sometimes the solutions include not only financial assistance but the actual loan of employees from other firms. Consensus and unity of purpose is standard Japanese practice for troubled companies. This practice also serves well for viable new projects and companies. Indeed, it is from such arrangements that ventures in high technology have come.

There is reason to believe that this may be changing as a result of Japanese companies becoming increasingly less dependent on their banks. Companies appear to be relying more on internal financing as well as making greater use of the market for their external requirement through independent security dealers. There is also the entry of foreign banks into the Japanese financial markets. Their entry promises to increase competition, which may eventually entice major Japanese companies from their main banks. There is also the growth of joint industrial ventures in the country, which has cast up the issue of divided loyalties to the banks of several companies.

The net result appears to be dissolution of the once strong ties between Japanese banks and industries —a process under way all over the world. Due to its consensus decision-making tradition, Japan may not be overwhelmed by the process.

Outside the United States, Europe, and Japan, Hong Kong and Singapore have the greatest concentration of banks and financial institutions. On occasion their sophistication exceeds that of London and New York. They have prospered because of convenience to the Asian mainland and islands by providing financial services including laundering money from such illegal activities as drugs and piracy. An educated labor force, many with English language skills, in Hong Kong and Singapore serve them well in meeting the requirements of international finance. All these factors are further reinforced by the inability of other Asian countries to put together a banking and financial organization capable of transferring capital from the industrialized countries and other areas to rapidly developing countries.

For their part, Singapore specializes in collecting and trading money. Hong Kong specializes in the syndication of loans to Asia because of closer connections to New York and London, as well as tax advantages. These activities complement each other. This may be changing as a result of Hong Kong's new relations with China and as the two Asian centers are competing for each other's business. This is understandable in view of the importance of financial services to national income in both.

Neither Singapore nor Hong Kong has a central bank. Self-regulation of financial institutions is apparently taken seriously in both city-states. In Singapore, for instance, a proposed merger of the Monetary Authority of Singapore, which supervised banks, and the Board of Commission of Currency, which is the city-state's note issues, for the purpose of establishing a central bank, was never carried through. Hong Kong has undertaken what some observers view as a vain attempt to control domestic inflation by taking its banks more firmly in hand. Hong Kong's situation may be made more difficult in the future due to its new "two-system" relation with China.

CHANGING PERCEPTIONS OF BANKERS

How have changes over the past few years affected bankers? It is difficult to say. It is simply difficult to gauge the full effect of these changes on bankers carrying out their day-to-day business. A number of observations can be made. One is that many bankers are becoming more risk conscious if not risk averse. They are taking a very close look into the books of their present prospective clients with the idea of lending less for shorter periods rather than more for longer periods.

Second, they are attempting to charge a market price for each of the services they offer, no longer are they willing as before to cross-subsidize some services to their clients.

Third, banks are carefully watching their exposure to various sectors of their countries' economies. Most banks have always considered themselves better able to judge the domestic economic situation than the foreign scene. This has been amply demonstrated since 1979. There is also an awareness on their part that by supporting ailing companies in a given sector they have made the situation difficult for healthy companies. Thus, there has been a tendency to restrict bank exposure to the whole sector irrespective of the merits of an individual firm.

Fourth, bankers now feel there is a limit to the extent they can support any given sector or industry of the economy. Indeed only banks, government, and employees typically can make financial concessions to keep afloat a sinking company.

Fifth, there is concern about adequacy of bank capital. Essentially the foundation on which a bank rests, capital is defined by regulators as stockholders' equity, together with such items as loan-loss reserves and debt convertible into stock. Regulators use capital to gauge the loan and securities losses into insolvency.

Capital, of course, is not an infallible guide to banking strength. More than 9,000 American banks failed in the 1930s even though their capital was 13 percent. In 1980 the average capital ratio at the seventeen big American multinational banks had deteriorated to 4.6 percent from 5.1 percent in 1977. In December 1981 the comptroller and the Federal Reserve Board decreed that all but a few banks should maintain capital ratios of at least 5 percent. The so-called Basle Accord called for internationally active banks by 1992 to have capital equal to 8 percent of their risk assets.

It is the implication of the new minimum capital requirements that are worrisome to banks. For instance, each $100 million in bank capital permits lending up to $22 billion at a 4.5 percent capital ratio, but an increase of half a percentage point in capital means lending must be $222 million less. According to some estimates it was largely by maintaining lower capital ratios that big banks could generate annual loan growth of 12.7 percent over the period 1979–1982. A higher capital ratio may slow down loan growth. It may also force banks to be more insistent that a loan provide a solid return and repayment prospects.

It is clear that the new and proposed capital rules will have important effects on the ongoing merger and consolidation in American (and fóreign) banking. Quite simply banks wishing to merge and buy other banks will need regulatory approval. To do so they must show the authorities a very good capital position to gain approval. There is also the fear held by some bankers that the new (and proposed) capital ratio requirements will be used to slow down the flow of credit to the economy if traditional methods prove ineffective.

Sixth, without technology banks indeed would be in very serious trouble. Technology allows banks to produce and market their products more cheaply. By the end of the 1990s probably most banks around the world and nearly all of the American banks have Internet sites. Technological advances now give banks a better sense of their overall position and their risk and the power to control them accordingly. Banks spend much on technology. Apart from personnel costs, technology is typical the biggest item in the budget and growing the fastest. The difficulty is that only the biggest banks can afford to spend on a scale that will keep them on the cutting edge of technology.

Finally, experience with industrial bailouts has brought about a closer tie between banks and industry. Their interest in seeing to it that a firm is profitable has brought about this closer tie. It has also increased bank expertise in various industries. On the other hand, there is a detectable drift in that for some banks and firms the desire for long-term growth has given way to the need for short-term survival. This is unfortunate indeed for future growth in many countries. Yet the problems themselves are also bringing about a new era of cooperation between bankers and their clients, which may very well overcome many of these difficulties.

NOTES

1.   See George Macesich, *World Banking and Finance: Cooperation Versus Conflict* (New York: Praeger, 1984).

2.   Ibid.

3.   See Joseph B. Cahill, "Bank One Establishes Internet Unit as Part of Plan to Use Web to Expand," *Wall Street Journal*, June 25, 1999: p A8.

4.   See the discussions in *The Economist* October 21, 1995: pp. 75–77; *The Economist* November 27, 1993: pp. 3–30; *The Economist* October 9, 1993: p. 22.

5.   See Dimitrije Dimitrijević and George Macesich, *Money and Finance in Contemporary Yugoslavia* (New York: Praeger, 1973); Dimitrije Dimitrijević and George Macesich, *Money and Finance in Contemporary Yugoslavia: A Comparative Analysis* (New York: Praeger, 1984); Richard Lang, George Macesich, and Dragomir Vojnić, eds., *Political Economy of Yugoslavia Since 1974* (Zagreb: Informator, 1982).

Chapter 9

The Euro and the Dollar

ANOTHER EMERGING WORLD CURRENCY?

It is only recently that people outside Europe began to pay attention to the euro. Most policymakers in the United States assumed the position that what was good for Europe was probably also good for the United States and the dollar. Japan and other Asian countries were too preoccupied with their own monetary and economic problems in the closing years of the twentieth century to worry about a new European currency. Indeed, the Europeans themselves were more concerned with the details of how the new single currency would operate within Europe to give much thought to its wider impact.

There is, however, general agreement that the euro will very likely be a major world currency next only to the dollar, and indeed the euro and the dollar in terms of the economic and monetary weight they represent are a close match. Thus, the euro and the eleven European countries it represents account for a GDP of almost $7 trillion in 1998 compared to more than $8 trillion for the United States and the dollar. Indeed, the euro countries account for more than 19 percent of international trade outside the euro area, which is slightly larger than the 17 percent accounted for by the United States. To be sure, money and capital markets are much smaller in Europe than in the United States.

Moreover, the American dollar's role in global trade and finance is far more significant than simple relative weight suggests. The dollar is the dominant currency in the world's trade and financial markets. In fact, the dollar accounts for more than 80 percent of all foreign exchange transactions, the German mark for about 30 percent, and the other European member currencies for little more than 20 percent. Much the same is true for the dollar's share in other financial and money markets including bank lending, international bond issuance, and its weight in international transactions also makes it a currency of choice for countries' official reserves. To be sure, in a number of these markets the dollar's share has slipped somewhat from earlier years.

The dollar's dominant position in international trade and finance has given the United States a number of benefits including seigniorage from dollars held abroad, liquidity discount on government debt, and the ability to finance America's current account deficits in dollars.

What are the prospects that Europe, due to the euro, could have the above benefits for itself? In good measure this depends on the speed with which Europe and its euro can grow their international role. This in turn depends on whether the euro will appreciate or depreciate in terms of the dollar. The answer usually depends on the optimism or pessimism of the observer. The optimists believe that the euro will be strong and stable and so able to challenge the dollar. The pessimists, on the other hand, argue that the euro must first establish a significant record if investors are to take it seriously. History suggests that long after Britain passed its economic and political prime the pound sterling continued as the currency of choice in world markets.

Moreover, the future of the euro depends also on the new European Central Bank (ECB) and its policies. ECB's treaty requirements focus on its obligations to pursue price stability and not necessarily the euro's exchange rate. If it appears that the euro area is a relatively closed economy like the United States and Japan, the ECB may well take a hands-off attitude toward the euro. Such a development concerns observers who see that with both the euro and dollar areas pursuing domestic goals a possibility exists for currency instability on the international scene. This concern fuels efforts for some formal international coordination among the dollar, euro, and yen as the world's main currencies.

Even on the domestic level the euro and the European Monetary Union (EMU) may face difficulty if economic policy brings about a recession (or worse). The entire project may be cast in doubt. EMU may also be too inflexible to cope with economic shocks on the local level. In practice countries with their own currencies are free to manipulate interest rates with a view of moving out of recession. Such a route is now closed for the EMU members with their single currency euro. All that remains for the members is national fiscal policy, and this route is limited owing to the EMU's Stability and Growth Pact, whereby member countries agree to holding budget deficits to 3 percent of GDP or less. Indeed, countries violating the agreement are to be fined according to the votes of other member countries unless their output has fallen by 2 percent or more in the year in question.

Many observers agree that serious flaws exist in the design of the EMU and in the euro. The constraints placed on the ECB, according to some analysts, along with little freedom in national fiscal policy, does not look encouraging for success of the EMU project. If the EMU were to overcome the flaws of its design and register economic success perhaps Europe's governments will move to closer political integration. Attempts to save a flawed EMU by political integration may simply cast in doubt the entire enterprise.

Some idea of difficulties that the EMU may face is suggested by the fact that France though committed to monetary union would prefer a more flexible union that would allow the EMU and perhaps even assist it to fight unemployment. In effect, this would require a reconstruction of the EMU through a change in the Maastricht Treaty criteria to promote employment and growth. Indeed, the monetary union does not require their perpetration through the Stability Pact. Some observers attribute the conservatism embodied in these documents to past and present devotion to the gold standard.

Macroeconomic stimulus for whatever its merits may not alone be enough to deal with Europe's unemployment and growth problems. Substantial microeconomic changes are needed to deal with the heavy burden of supply-side problems. These are changes that are politically difficult to deal with when unemployment is high and electorates suspicious of any threat to their safety nets.

There is also the outstanding issue of EU enlargement. Prospective members in Eastern Europe and countries that have declined to take part such as Britain, Sweden, and Denmark may well present problems to the EMU. If the EMU works badly, Britain and the other "outs" are not likely to join. Eastern European countries may in any case not be ready for a long time. They are still struggling with the legacy of socialism. Whatever arrangements are made for the "outs" and prospective candidates some form of monetary cooperation will be required.

For instance, suppose the euro strengthens against other European currencies and so putting EMU members at a competitive disadvantage in trade. Such a situation may well bring about objections on the part of member countries particularly if growth in EMU is slowing while output is expanding elsewhere.

In fact, the potential for clashes in a conflicting patchwork of national and regional interests plagues Europe. The euro's performance will likely pit politicians against ECB, some arguing that a weak euro could help promote Europe's exports. ECB for its part insists that weakness of the euro should be avoided. The "Big 5" of the EU continue to press for preservation of their respective advantages; France fights to preserve its farm subsidies; Britain to preserve the EU annual budget rebate it won in 1984; Italy is expected to increase its net payments; Spain fights to save its inflow of EU aid; and Germany wants to reduce its high euro annual EU net payment.

To be sure the ECB has been given a high degree of independence, which is viewed as essential to the credibility of the EMU. However, the Stability and Growth Pact, although it provides a strict framework for fiscal convergence and stability, sets no binding rules for member states that stay within these limits. There is, moreover, considerable skepticism about the ability and willingness of EU authorities to strictly enforce the sanction and fines on a country facing serious economic difficulties already perhaps penalized in higher interest rates. Since sanctions are not automatic and require majority approval by participating member countries, the entire process may very quickly become politicized undermining the accountability and transparency of enforcement. Indeed, the credibility of the EMU would be cast in doubt as we noted.

Moreover, there is also the difficulty of the so-called free rider problem. Member states may not be particularly enthusiastic about providing necessary fiscal stimulus or restraint if a large part of the benefit would go to other countries or if their fiscal positions are already satisfactory in their view.

Clearly, some arrangement for fiscal coordination within the EMU must be made in the event of difficulties. For instance, in case of a severe recession in the EU region, or a supply shock, the envisaged policy response by the ECB through monetary policy focused as it is on price stability may simply be inappropriate. Discretionary fiscal policy measures may then become necessary.

Of course, more effective fiscal policy coordination among member states may well deal with the short-run problems. Over the long run, however, decentralized fiscal policies may not be able to provide the degree of macroeconomic stabilization required by the EMU area. It has been suggested that the EU create a central fiscal authority and provide it adequate resources to conduct necessary stabilization policies particularly if European integration grows.

In reality, the EU has a long way to go to meet the way a federation handles fiscal policies in the matter of allocation, redistribution, and stabilization. These functions are carried out largely by central governments with varying degrees of participation from various levels of government. Federations handle such matters by transfers mostly from central to regional levels of government. As a result of increasing the dependency on the part of regional governments the effective degree of financial and fiscal centralization is increased.

The EU is simply less centralized than a federation. It remains to be seen whether the EMU policy framework embodied in the Maastricht Treaty and the Stability and Growth Pact will be able to carry out fiscal policy effectively or whether more centralization will be required to deal with the issues of stabilization and redistribution.

It should be underscored that the EMU was launched during a favorable cyclical upswing. If the economy should be hit by a cyclical downturn economic and perhaps political difficulties may well engulf the EU. If these difficulties are to be avoided the drive for closed EU political integration and thus more centralization of fiscal policy may well be in the cards for the euro area. Certainly the current EU fiscal framework, which relies exclusively on exchange of information, publicity, and peer pressure will be able to deal with the ensuring problems. Political integration may come to Europe as a by-product to problems with the existing fiscal policy arrangements. Failure to do so may, in the long term, simply end in the dissolution of the EU, the EMU, and the euro area.

WHY A SINGLE CURRENCY?

Given the difficulties confronting the EU why have a single currency at all? One possible answer has been given by Robert Mundell.[1] His answer draws on the theory of optimal currency areas. In effect, the optimal area for a common currency to be used depends on the degree to which real resources can be transferred within it in response to shocks. According to Mundell the issue depends on the mobility of capital and labor. If these factors can move easily from a depressed area within the common currency zone to a more prosperous one, the zone should continue to use a common currency. If not, the depressed area should be allowed to depreciate its local currency relative to the rest of the zone. This would stimulate local demand for its idle capital and labor and thus make its products cheaper relative to the rest of the zone. At the same time imports from the rest of the zone would be more expensive thereby decreasing local demand for output from the rest of the zone. The net effect would be to help spread the effects of the shock to the local area's trading partners.

Another variation to the theme of optimal currency areas is provided by Ronald McKinnon who argues that if the local area is already open to trade with the rest of the currency zone, then local capital and labor would realize that devaluation had reduced their real returns and wages. They would raise their nominal rates of return and wages enough so as to cancel out the effects of devaluation. Accordingly, the size of the optimum currency area depends on the intensity of trade within it.

Of course a third way to soften the shocks on the local area is by fiscal transfers within the common currency zone. This is done, for instance, in the United States and in most other industrial countries. As stated above the EU does appear to have a desire to do the same though it remains to be seen whether there is the political will to go along with the significant fiscal transfers required in many areas of EU. In any case, given the limited resources at the EU's disposal it is unlikely that the EU would be able to make significant fiscal transfers that might be required in the face of a shock that reduced income in just one of the smaller countries.[2]

Most observers agree that European countries fail both in terms of mobility of labor and capital and in terms of fiscal transfers.[3] They also agree and cite evidence in support that European labor markets are more rigid than those in the United States. Shocks caused by the currency union would very likely last a long time owing to the fact that wages would be very slow to adjust. All of this is further confirmed by the high rates of unemployment in Europe. The conclusion is that only in terms of openness and intensity of trade relations do EU countries qualify as comprising an optimum currency area. It is likely that smaller countries within the EU will benefit by a common currency with their trading partners, and small countries outside the EU that find their trade carried out predominantly with one or more large countries within the EU would do well to join in the common currency.

For all its attractiveness to many people, the euro is still the only international currency in history that does not have a strong central state, nor a metallic backing. The experiment flies in the face of historical experience that political union precedes economic union and a single currency. The EU apparently hopes to be the exception. At the center of the EMU is the ECB, modeled after the German central bank and charged with maintaining a noninflationary monetary policy. The ECB is analogous to the Federal Reserve Board of Governors, while Europe's national central banks become counterparts to the regional banks in the United States.

As discussed above, it is the Europeans great wish that a strong euro will rival the dollar as an international reserve currency and thus make the EU an important player on the international scene. This may or may not happen. To be sure, the EU is one of the world's largest trading regions, over 80 percent of its trade is within Europe. Few observers are confident that the EMU will open up trade and capital markets to non-European trade and investment. Until such an opening takes place Europe and the role of its euro as an international reserve currency will be limited at best.

Even as the euro is inaugurated conflict has arisen over the EU's budget especially in agricultural subsidies and over the amounts paid by each country. Moreover, the Germans, in particular, are pressing for European rules setting minimum tax rates. Their hope is that such tax rates would reduce the risk of Germany's losing economically to tax-attractive countries as Ireland and others in the EU. The boom in Ireland during the 1990s owes much to a powerful mix of reducing tax rates and cutting public expenditure.

These and related conflicts in Europe will very likely grow due to the lack of sufficiently flexible wages and prices, inability of workers and compensatory fiscal mechanism among members of the EMU. Shocks that could be easily handled by exchange rate changes will very likely be converted into serious political issues. There is good reason to expect that the EMU will concentrate responsibility for solutions to Europe's problems in fewer and probably less accountable hands.

Anna J. Schwartz suggests what the new ECB can learn from the experience of the U.S. Federal Reserve System.[4] She suggests that the ECB adopt the current Federal Reserve System's "steady-as-you-go" approach and its management of banking crises. But it should avoid the Federal Reserve System's blunders. Schwartz underscores these errors as "too little, too late"; "too much, too often"; "stop-and-go"; and "open mouth." These past policies of the Federal Reserve System have not brought about desired results. There is little doubt that the ECB has much to learn from the turbulent history of the Federal Reserve System. True enough, the ECB also has no historical precedent. As Schwartz points out, EMU members have in effect "thrown away the key and committed themselves to the euro and the policies of the ECB." The outcome, indeed, cannot be predicted.

The European visionaries great desire was that a strong EU-wide currency will rival the dollar as an international rescue currency helping to make Europe an economic giant in the global economy. This, in turn, they envision will lead to the formulation of a political and security union in Europe. In this they may well have placed the cart before the horse by insisting on economic and monetary union before political union. Milton Friedman put it well when he noted that "monetary union imposed under unfavorable conditions will prove a barrier to the achievement of political unity."[5]

For an overtaxed and overregulated EMU mired in social welfare problems, Europe has its problems that single currency may not be able to address effectively. Countries still in control of most economic and social policies will continue to grow at different rates. If they are unable to alter exchange rates, unemployment and eventually declining wage rates will become the necessary adjustment means. It should come as no surprise that political reaction will occur as a result. This will serve to undermine whatever progress is made toward European union.

The international implications for a euro-dollar world have been underscored by various writers.[6] If confidence in the ECB is established there may well be diversification from the dollar to the euro. Some countries may well opt to keep part of their reserves in euros. If the EMU is successful it may provoke the formation of an Asian monetary union pushed by Japan, China, and other Asian countries. The world will have alternative assets to the dollar to use in international reserves as a by-product. In itself, this is an attractive option to other countries if any one of the three leading currencies lean toward instability.

The ECB is cast to play a singularly critical role with EMU. Although designed to be independent from political pressure, the ECB is having a tough time guarding its status from European politicians pushing their own views of interest rates and related issues. It is thus not surprising that not everyone agrees that central bank independence is a good thing, and there is evidence that raises doubt.[7] One piece of evidence suggests that the supposed correlation between central-bank independence and low inflation is suspect. Even if correct, the "credibility" issue that goes with the argument for independence may not hold. It is difficult, so the argument goes, to objectively define "independence." Sometimes one or another definition is used. Other studies do find such a correlation.

The received central bank argument that independence increases credibility and credibility reduces the cost of getting inflation down may not be correct. Evidence suggests that central bank independence fails to reduce the cost of disinflation and may actually increase it. Indeed, in countries with relatively independent central banks, the record suggests that this is in fact the case. Again, the problem may be in the proper definition of "independence." Of course other possibilities including independence and low inflation are jointly the result of some third factor such as society's willingness to tolerate high inflation.[8] Also it may well be that central bankers are less sensitive to unemployment than politicians. In any event, the ECB is designed to be the most "independent" in the world and in time the EMU and the rest of the world can judge the results.

Some members of the EMU expect great things from a single currency. Others are not sure what the future may bring. Germany hopes that a single currency will reduce European tensions. Spain looks toward a reduction in regional economic disparity. France hopes that the euro will become an important counterweight to the dollar. Britain tends to look at the euro as a threat to its own exceptionalism. Italy apparently sees the euro as a means for bringing about order in its own monetary and financial affairs.

A single currency will have an important benefit particularly in improving the transparency and efficiency of a single European market. On this score, individual investors will be able to better judge the value of investments. It is not clear that a single European currency and monetary union before a true political union will do much for real or imagined problems and insecurities that many Europeans have.

It also may well be that in the final analysis the case for the EMU is political. One senses that many European leaders view monetary union as desirable because it will contribute to a European political union. If the EMU and the euro fail, European political union may indeed be set back with little future prospects.

Whether the EMU will open up trade and capital markets to non-European trade and investment is doubtful. Until such an opening occurs, the role of the euro as an international reserve currency—and of the European Union as an economic power will be limited. In fact, it may be tempting for the Europeans to mimic the "benign neglect" they have often accused Americans of following for the dollar. Some observers hold that, with the euro and dollar concentrating exclusively on domestic concerns, world currency instability might increase. This is a lesson that should have been learned from the 1930s when the dollar and pound were two semi-dominant currencies.

NOTES

1. Robert Mundell, "The Case for the Euro-I," *Wall Street Journal,* March 24, 1998: A22 and Robert Mundell, "The Case for the Euro-II," *Wall Street Journal,* March 25, 1998: A22. Robert Mundell, "Making the Euro Work," *Wall Street Journal*, April 30, 1998: A22.

2. See for instance the discussion in Larry Neal and Daniel Barbezat, *The Economics of the European Union and the Economies of Europe* (New York, and Oxford: Oxford University Press, 1998), Chap.7; especially Peter Kenen, *Monetary Union in Europe: Moving Beyond Maastricht* (Cambridge: Cambridge University Press, 1995); Daniel Gros and Niels Thuygesen, *European Monetary Integration* (New York: St. Martin's Press, 1992); Paul de Grauwe, *The Economics of Monetary Integration* (Oxford: Oxford University Press, 1992).

3. See Neal and Barbezat, *The Economics of the European Union*, pp. 144–170.

4. Anna J. Schwartz, "What Europe Can Learn from the Fed," *Wall Street Journal*, December 31, 1998: A10.

5. Milton Friedman, "Whither the EMU?," *Wall Street Journal*, June 20, 1997: A20.

6. See for instance, Mundell, "The Case for the Euro-II" *Wall Street Journal*, March 25, 1998: A22.

7. *The Economist* 350, no. 8108, February 27–March 5, 1999: 76.

8. Ibid.

Selected Bibliography

Alpert, Paul. *Twentieth-Century Economic History of Europe*. New York: Henry Schuman, 1951.

Angell, James W. "Appropriate Monetary Policies and Operations in the United States Today." *Review of Economics and Statistics* 42 (August 1960): 247–252.

Arndt, H. W. *The Economic Lessons of the Nineteen-Thirties*. London: Frank Cass, 1963.

Arnold, Roger A. "Hayek and Institutional Evolution." *Journal of Libertarian Studies* 4, no. 4 (fall 1980): 341–352.

Attiyeh, Richard. "Rules versus Discretion: A Comment." *Journal of Political Economy* 73 (April 1965): 170–172.

Auerback, Robert D. *Money, Banking, and Financial Markets*. New York: Macmillan, 1982.

Beck, Nathaniel. "Presidential Influence on the Federal Reserve in the 1970s." *American Journal of Political Science* (August 1982): 415–445.

Bloomfield, Arthur L. *Monetary Policy under the International Gold Standard: 1880–1914*. New York: Federal Reserve Bank of New York, 1959.

Bonn, Moritz J. *The Crumbling of Empire: The Disintegration of World Economy*. London: Allen & Unwin, 1938.

Bordo, M. D. "The Classical Gold Standard: Source Lessons for Today." Federal Reserve Bank of St. Louis, *Monthly Review* (May 1981): 2–17.

Brennan, H. Geoffrey, and James M. Buchanan. *Monopoly in Money and Inflation: The Case of a Constitution to Discipline Government.* London: Institute of Economic Affairs, 1981.

Bronfenbrenner, Martin. "Statistical Tests of Rival Monetary Rules." *Journal of Political Economy* 69 (February 1961): 1–14.

Cagan, Phillip. *Determinants and Effects of Changes in the Money Stock, 1875–1960.* New York: Columbia University Press, 1965.

Cameron, Rondo with collaboration of Olga Crisp, Hugh T. Patrick, and Richard Tilly. *Banking in the Early Stages of Industrialization: A Study in Comparative Economic History.* New York: Oxford University Press, 1967.

Catterall, R.C.H. *The Second Bank of the United States.* Chicago: University of Chicago Press, 1903.

Champ, B. and S. Freeman. *Modeling Monetary Economies.* New York: J. Wiley, 1994.

Clapham, John H. "Europe after the Great Wars, 1816 and 1820." *Economic Journal* (December 1920): 423–435.

———. *The Bank of England.* Cambridge: Cambridge University Press, 1958.

Day, John P. *Introduction to World Economic History since the Great War.* London: Macmillan, 1939.

de Grauwe D. *The Economics of Monetary Integration.* Oxford: Oxford University Press, 1992.

Dewey, D. R. *The Second United States Bank.* Washington, D.C.: U.S. Government Printing Office, 1910.

Downs, Anthony. *Inside Bureaucracy.* Boston: Little, Brown and Company, 1967.

Fisher, Irving. *Stabilizing the Dollar.* New York: Macmillan, 1920.

Frankel, S. Herbert, *Two Philosophies of Money: The Conflict of Trust and Authority.* New York: St. Martin's Press, 1977. *Money and Liberty.* Washington, D.C.: American Enterprise Institute for Public Policy Research, 1980.

Friedman, Milton. "A Monetary and Fiscal Framework for Economic Stability." *American Economic Review* 38 (June 1948): 245–264.

———. "Commodity Reserve Currency." *Journal of Political Economy* 59 (June 1951): 203–232.

———. "Price, Income, and Monetary Changes in Three Wartime Periods." *American Economic Review, Papers and Proceedings* (May 1952): 612–625.

———. "The Quantity Theory of Money—A Restatement." In *Studies in the Quantity Theory of Money,* edited by Milton Friedman. Chicago: University of Chicago Press, 1956.

———. "The Demand for Money—Some Theoretical and Empirical Results." *Journal of Political Economy* 67 (June 1959): 327–351.

———. *A Program for Monetary Stability.* The Millar Lectures, no. 3. New York: Fordham University Press, 1960.

———. "The Lag in Effect of Monetary Policy." *Journal of Political Economy* 69 (October 1961): 447–466.

————. "Should There Be an Independent Monetary Authority?" In *In Search of a Monetary Constitution*, edited by L. B. Yeager. Cambridge, Mass.: Harvard University Press, 1962.

————. "The Role of Monetary Policy." *American Economic Review* 58 (March 1968): 1–17.

————. *The Optimum Quantity of Money and Other Essays.* Chicago: Aldine, 1969.

————. *The Quantity Theory of Money and Other Essays.* Chicago: Aldine, 1969.

————. "Monetary Policy: Theory and Practice." *Journal of Money, Credit, and Banking* (February 1982).

————. "The Keynes Centenary: A Monetarist Reflects." *The Economist* (June 4, 1983): 17–18.

————. *Money Mischief: Episodes in Monetary History.* New York and San Diego: Harcourt Brace Jovanovich, 1992.

————. "Whither the EMU?" *Wall Street Journal* (June 20, 1997): A20.

————, ed. *Studies in the Quantity Theory of Money.* Chicago: University of Chicago Press, 1956.

Friedman, Milton, and Rose D. Friedman. *Two Lucky People: Memoirs.* Chicago: University of Chicago Press, 1998.

Friedman, Milton, and Anna J. Schwartz. *A Monetary History of the United States, 1867–1960.* National Bureau of Economic Research. Studies in Business Cycles. No. 12. Princeton: Princeton University Press, 1963.

————. *Monetary Trends in the United States and United Kingdom: Their Relation to Income, Prices, and Interest Rates, 1867–1975.* Chicago: University of Chicago Press, 1982.

Galbraith, J. K. *The Great Crash.* Boston: Houghton Mifflin, 1972.

Goldfeld, Stephen M. "New Monetary Control Procedures." *Journal of Money, Credit and Banking* (February 1982): 148–155.

Gordon, George J. *Public Administration in America.* 2d ed. New York: St. Martin's Press, 1982.

Gramley, Lyle E. "Guidelines for Monetary Policy: The Case against Simple Rules." *Readings in Money, National Income, and Stabilization Policy,* edited by W. L. Smith and R. L. Teigen, rev. ed. Homewood, Ill.: Irwin, 1970: 488–493.

Gregory, Theodore E. "Rationalization and Technological Unemployment." *Economic Journal* (December 1930): 441–467.

———— "The Economic Significance of Gold Maldistribution." *Manchester School of Economics and Social Studies* 2 (1931): 77–85.

————. *Gold, Unemployment, and Capitalism.* London: P. S. King, 1933.

————. *The Gold Standard and Its Future.* 3d ed. New York: Dutton, 1935.

Gros, Daniel, and Niels Thuygesen. *European Monetary Integration.* New York: St. Martin's Press, 1992.

Guillebaud, Claude W. *The Economic Recovery of Germany from 1933 to the Incorporation of Austria in March, 1938.* London: Macmillan, 1939.

Hammond, Bray. *Banks and Politics in America.* Princeton: Princeton University Press, 1957.

Hammond, Daniel J., ed. *The Legacy of Milton Friedman as Teacher.* Cheltenham, Glos., U.K.: Edward Elgar, 1999.

Hart, Albert G. "The Chicago Plan for Banking Reform." *Review of Economic Studies* 2 (1935): 104–116.

———. "The Role of Monetary Policy." *American Economic Review* (March 1968): 1–17.

Havrilesky, Thomas M. "The Economist's Corner: The Politicization of Monetary Policy." *Bankers Magazine* (spring 1975): 101–104.

Havrilesky, Thomas M., and John T. Boorman, eds. *Current Issues in Monetary Theory and Policy.* 2d ed. Arlington Heights, Ill.: AHM Publishing Company, 1980.

Hayek, Friedrich A. *Studies in Philosophy, Politics, and Economics.* Chicago: University of Chicago Press, 1967.

———. *Denationalization of Money.* London: Institute for Economic Affairs, 1976.

———. "The Keynes Centenary: The Austrian Critique." *The Economist* (June 11, 1983): 41.

Hearn, Daniel S. *Federal Reserve Policy Reappraised, 1951–1959.* New York: Columbia University Press, 1963.

Hein, Scott E. "Dynamic Forecasting and the Demand for Money." *Federal Reserve Bank of St. Louis Review* (June/July 1980): 13–23.

Hendershoot, P. H., and F. DeLeeuw. "Free Reserves, Interest Rates and Deposits: A Synthesis." *Journal of Finance* 25 (June 1970): 599–614.

Hicks, John R. "The Keynes Centenary: A Skeptical Follower." *The Economist* (June 18, 1983): 17–19.

Hirsch, Fred. *Social Limits to Growth.* Cambridge, Mass.: Harvard University Press, 1976.

Hirschman, Albert. "Rival Interpretations of Market Society: Civilizing, Destructive, or Feeble?" *Journal of Economic Literature* (December 1982): 1463–1484.

Hoover, Calvin B. *Memories of Capitalism, Communism, and Nazism.* Durham, N.C.: Duke University Press, 1965.

Hoskins, W. Lee. "Defending Zero Inflation: All for Naught." Federal Reserve Bank of Minneapolis. *Quarterly Review* (spring 1991): 16–20.

Hutchinson, Keith. *The Decline and Fall of British Capitalism.* New York: Scribner's, 1950.

"Is the Federal Reserve's Monetary Control Policy Misdirected?" *Journal of Money, Credit, and Banking* (February 1982): 119–147.

Jenks, L. H. *The Migrations of British Capital to 1875.* New York: A. A. Knopf, 1927.

Johnson, E., ed. *The Collected Writings John Maynard Keynes.* Vol. 17, *Activities 1920–1922: Treaty Revision and Reconstruction.* Vol. 18, *Activities 1922–1932: The End of Reparations.* New York and London: Macmillan and Cambridge University Press, 1977, 1978, respectively, for the Royal Economic Society.

Johnson, Harry G. *Macroeconomics and Monetary Theory.* London: Gray-Mills, 1971.

Kahn, Alfred E. *Great Britain in the World Economy.* New York: Columbia University Press, 1946.

Kareken, J. H., and N. Wallace, eds. *Models of Monetary Economics.* Minneapolis: Federal Reserve Bank of Minneapolis, 1980.

Kenen, Peter. *Monetary Union in Europe: Moving Beyond Maastricht.* Cambridge: Cambridge University Press, 1995.

Keynes, John M. "The Economics of War in Germany." *Economic Journal* (September 1914): 442–452.

———. "War and the Financial System, August 14, 1914." *Economic Journal* (September 1914): 460–486.

———. "The City of London and the Bank of England, August 1914." *Quarterly Journal of Economics* (November 1914): 48–71.

———. *The Economic Consequences of the Peace.* London: Macmillan, 1920.

———. *A Revision of the Treaty.* London: Macmillan, 1922.

———. *Monetary Reform.* London: Harcourt Brace, 1924.

———. *The Economic Consequences of Mr. Churchill.* London: Leonard and Virginia Woolf, 1925.

———. *The End of Laissez-Faire.* London: Leonard and Virginia Woolf, 1927.

———. "The French Stabilization Law." *Economic Journal* (September 1928): 490–494.

———. "The German Transfer Problem." *Economic Journal* (March 1929): 107.

———. *A Treatise in Money.* vol. 1. London: Macmillian, 1930.

———. *Essays in Persuasion.* New York: Harcourt, Brace, 1932.

———. *The General Theory of Employment, Interest, and Money.* New York: Harcourt Brace, 1936.

———. "Theory of the Rate of Interest." Reprinted in W. Feller and B. F. Healey, eds. *Readings in the Theory of Income Distribution.* Philadelphia: Blaxiston, 1949.

———. *The General Theory of Employment, Interest, and Money.* New York: Harcourt, Brace & World, 1964.

Keynes, John M., and H. D. Henderson. *Can Lloyd George Do It? An Examination of the Liberal Pledge.* London: Nation and Athenaeum, 1919.

Keynes, Milo, ed. *Essays on John Maynard Keynes.* New York: Cambridge University Press, 1975.

Kindleberger, Charles. *The World in Depression, 1929–1939.* Berkeley: University of California Press, 1973.

————. *A Financial History of Western Europe.* 2nd ed. New York: Oxford University Press, 1993.

Klein, Benjamin. "The Competitive Supply of Money." *Journal of Money, Credit, and Banking* (November 1974).

Kydland, Finn, and Edward Prescott. "Rules Rather than Discretion: The Inconsistency of Optimal Plans." *Journal of Political Economy* 3 (1977).

————. "Rules v. Discretion." *The Economist* (March 2, 1991): 71–72.

Laidler, D. *The Demand for Money: Theories and Evidence.* Scranton, Penn.: International Textbook, 1969: 106–97.

————. Review of *Two Philosphies of Money.* Journal of Economic Literature (June 1979): 570–572.

————. "The Bullionist Controversy." In *Money,* edited by John Eatwell, Murray Milgate, Peter Newman. New York: W. W. Norton Co., 1989): 60–70.

League of Nations. *The Network of World Trade.* Geneva: League of Nations, annually 1932–1944.

Lerner, Abba P. "Milton Friedman's 'A Program for Monetary Stability': A Review." *Journal of the American Statistical Association* 57 (March 1962): 211–220. Reprinted in *Monetary Policy: The Argument from Keynes' Treatise to Friedman,* edited by William Hamovitch. Boston: Heath, 1966.

Macesich, George. "The Source of Monetary Disturbances in the United States, 1834–1845." *Journal of Economic History* (September 1960): 407–434.

————. "International Trade and U.S. Economic Development Revisited." *Journal of Economic History* (September 1961): 384–385.

————. "The Quantity Theory and the Income Expenditure Theory in an Open Economy: Canada 1926–1958." *Canadian Journal of Economics and Political Science* (August 1964): 368–390.

————. *Commercial Banking and Regional Development in the United States, 1950–1960.* Tallahassee: Florida State University Press, 1965.

————. "International Trade and United States Economic Development Revisited." Reprinted in Stanley Cohen and Forest Hill, eds. *American Economic History.* Philadelphia: Lippincott, 1966.

————. "Central Banking, Monetary Policy, and Economic Activity." U.S. Congress. House. Subcommittee on Domestic Finance of the Committee on Banking and Currency. *Compendium on Monetary Policy Guidelines and Federal Reserve Structure.* 90th Cong., 2d Sess. Washington, D.C.: U.S. Government Printing Office, December 1968.

————. "Stock and the Federal Reserve System." U.S. Congress. House. Subcommittee on Domestic Finance of the Committee on Banking and Currency. *Compendium on Monetary Policy Guidelines and Federal Reserve Structure.* 90th Cong., 2d sess. Washington, D.C.: U.S. Government Printing Office, December 1968.

————. *Geldpolitik in einem gemeinsametz europaischen markt* (Money in a European common market). Baden-Baden: Nomos Verlagsgesellschaft, 1972.

————. "Monetary Policy in the Common Market Countries: Rules versus Discretion." *Weltwirtschaftliches Archives* 198 (1972): 20–52.

————. "Monetary Policy and International Interdependence in the Great Depression: The U.S. and Yugoslavia." *Zbornik.* Belgrade: Serbian Academy of Sciences and Arts, 1976.

————. *The International Monetary Economy and the Third World.* New York: Praeger, 1981.

————. *Monetarism: Theory and Policy.* New York: Praeger, 1983.

————. *The Politics of Monetarism: Its Historical and Institutional Development.* Totowa, N.J.: Rowman and Allanheld, 1984.

————. *Economic Nationalism and Stability.* New York: Praeger, 1985.

————. *Monetary Policy and Politics: Rules Versus Discretion.* Westport, Conn. and London: Praeger, 1992.

————. *The United States Economic in the Changing Global Economy: Policy Implications and Issues.* Westport, Conn.: Praeger, 1997.

————. *Political Economy of Money: Emerging Fiat Monetary Regime.* Westport, Conn.: Greenwood, 1999.

Macesich, George, and F. A. Close. "Comparative Stability of Monetary Velocity and the Investment Multiplier for Austria and Yugoslavia." *Florida State University Slavic Papers.* Vol. 3. Tallahassee: Florida State University, 1969.

Macesich, George, and Hui-Liang Tsai. *Money in Economic Systems.* New York: Praeger, 1982.

Mayer, Thomas. "The Lag in Effect of Monetary Policy: Some Criticisms." *Western Economic Journal 5* (September 1967): 324–342.

————. Statement. *Compendium:* 46–72. "Stock and the Federal Reserve System." U.S. Congress. House. Subcommittee on Domestic Finance of the Committee on Banking and Currency. *Compendium on Monetary Policy Guidelines and Federal Reserve Structure.* 90th Cong., 2d sess. Washington, D.C.: U.S. Government Printing Office, December 1968.

McCloskey, Donald N., and J. Richard Zecher. "How the International Gold Standard Worked 1880–1913." In *The Monetary Approach to the Balance of Payments,* edited by Jacob A. Frankel and Harry G. Johnson. Toronto: University of Toronto Press, 1976.

Meigs, A. J. *Free Reserves and the Money Supply.* Chicago: University of Chicago Press, 1962.

Meiselman, David, ed. *Varieties of Monetary Experience.* Chicago: University of Chicago Press, 1970.

Meltzer, Allen H. Introduction. *Compendium*: 488–491. "Stock and the Federal Reserve System." U.S. Congress. House. Subcommittee on Domestic Finance of the Committee on Banking and Currency. *Compendium on Monetary Policy Guidelines and Federal Reserve Structure.* 90th Cong., 2d sess. Washington, D.C.: U.S. Government Printing Office, December 1968.

Mints, Lloyd W. *Monetary Policy for a Competitive Society.* New York: McGraw-Hill, 1950.

————. "Monetary Policy and Stabilization." *American Economic Review, Papers and Proceedings* 41 (May 1951): 188–193.

Modigliani, Franco. "Some Empirical Tests of Monetary Management and of Rules versus Discretion." *Journal of Political Economy* 72 (June 1964): 211–245.

Moggridge, Donald, ed. *Collected Writings* [Keynes]. *Activities, 1940–1943: External War Finance* [Keynes]. New York: Cambridge University Press, 1979.

Morrell, S. O. "In Search of a New Monetary Order: An Open Discussion on Aspects of a Freely Competitive Monetary Arrangement." *Institute Scholar* 1, no. 1 (1980): 1–2.

Mundell, Robert. "The Case for the Euro-I." *Wall Street Journal* (March 24, 1998): A22.

————. "The Case for the Euro-II." *Wall Street Journal* (March 25, 1998): A22.

————. "Making the Euro Work." *Wall Street Journal* (April 30, 1998): A22.

Neal, Larry, and Daniel Barbezat. *The Economics of the European Union and the Economies of Europe*. New York and Oxford: Oxford University Press, 1998.

New Monetary Control Procedures. Federal Reserve Staff Study. Vols. 1 and 2. Washington, D.C.: Board of Governors of the Federal Reserve System, February 1982.

Niles' *Weekly Register* 34: 154.

Nordhaus, William. "Creeping Economic Constitutionalism." *New York Times* (December 27, 1981).

North, D.C. *The Economic Growth of the United States, 1790–1860*. Englewood Cliffs, N.J.: Prentice-Hall, 1961.

Nurkse, Ragnar. *International Currency Experience*. Geneva: League of Nations, 1944.

Ohlin, Bertil. *International and Interregional Trade*. Cambridge, Mass.: Harvard University Press, 1935.

Okun, Arthur M. *The Political Economy of Prosperity*. Washington, D.C.: Brookings Institute, 1970.

Pierce, James L. "The Myth of Congressional Supervision of Monetary Policy." *Journal of Monetary Economics* (April 1978). Reprinted in Thomas M. Havrilesky and John T. Boorman, eds. *Current Issues in Monetary Theory and Policy*. 2d ed. Arlington Heights, Ill.: AHM Publishing Company, 1980.

Pigou. Arthur C. *Aspects of British Economic History, 1918–1925*. New York: Macmillan, 1947.

Roskill, Stephen. *Hankey: Man of Secrets, 1919–1931*. Vol. 2. S.D. 16. 23d Cong., 1st sess. Annapolis: U.S. Naval Institute Press, 1972.

Rothbard, Murray. *The Mystery of Banking*. New York: Richardson and Snyder, 1983: 179–190.

Samuelson, Paul A. "Reflections on Central Banking." *National Banking Review* I (September 1963): 15–28.

Sargent, T. J. *Dynamic Macroeconomic Theory*. Cambridge, Mass.: Harvard University Press, 1987.

Scheiber, Harry N. "The Pet Banks in Jacksonian Politics and Finance, 1833–1841." *Journal of Economic History* (June 1963): 196–214.

Schlesinger, Arthur M., Jr. *Age of Jackson.* Boston: Little, Brown and Company, 1945.

Schneider, Erich. "Automatism or Discretion in Monetary Policy." *Banca Nationale del Lavoro Quarterly Review* 23 (June 1970): 3–19.

Schotta, Charles, Jr. "The Performance of Alternative Monetary Rules in Canada, 1927–1961." *National Banking Review* 1 (December 1963): 221–227.

Schumpeter, Joseph. *Capitalism, Socialism, and Democracy.* New York: Harper, 1942.

Schwartz, Anna J. "Short-Term Targets of Three Central Banks." In *Targets and Indicators of Monetary Policy,* edited by Karl Brummer. San Francisco: Chandler, 1969.

———. "A Review of Explanations of 1929–1933." In *FSU Proceedings and Reports,* edited by George Macesich. Vols. 12–13. Tallahassee: Florida State University, 1978–1979.

———. "Empirical Findings of the Study of Monetary Trends in the United States and United Kingdom." *FSU Proceedings and Reports,* edited by George Macesich. Vol. 15. Tallahassee: Florida State University/Center for Yugoslav-American Studies, Research, and Exchanges, 1981.

———. "The U.S. Gold Commission and the Resurgence of Interest in a Return to the Gold Standard." *FSU Proceedings and Reports,* edited by George Macesich. Vol. 17. Tallahassee: Florida State University/Center for Yugoslav-American Studies, Research, and Exchanges, 1983.

———. "Banking School, Currency School, Free Banking School." In *Money,* edited by John Eatwell, Murray Milgate, Peter Newman. New York: W. W. Norton, Co., 1989: 41–49.

———. "What Europe Can Learn from the Fed." *Wall Street Journal* (December 31, 1998): A10.

Simmel, Georg. *The Philosophy of Money.* Translated by T. Bottomore and D. Frisby. Introduction by D. Frisby. London: Routledge and Kegan Paul, 1978.

Simons, Henry C. "A Positive Program for Laissez-Faire: Some Proposals for a Liberal Economic Policy." *Public Policy Pamphlet.* No. 15, edited by H. D. Gideonse. Chicago: University of Chicago Press, 1934.

———. "Rules versus Authorities in Monetary Policy." *Journal of Political Economy* 44 (February 1936): 1–30.

———. "The Requisites of Free Competition." *American Economic Review,* Supplement 26 (March 1936): 69.

———. *Economic Policy for a Free Society.* Chicago: University of Chicago Press, 1948.

Smith, Lawrence. "England's Return to the Gold Standard in 1925." *Journal of Economic and Business History* (February 1932): 228–258.

Smith, Lawrence, and John W. L. Winder. "Price and Interest Rate Expectations and the Demand for Money in Canada." *Journal of Finance* (June 1979): 671–682.

Smith, W. B. *Economic Aspects of the Second Bank of the United States.* Cambridge, Mass.: Harvard University Press, 1953.

Snyder, Carl. "The Problem of Monetary and Economic Stability." *Quarterly Journal of Economics* 49 (February 1935): 198.

————. *Capitalism the Creator: The Economic Foundations of Modern Industrial Society.* New York: Macmillan, 1940.

Spencer, R. "Inflation, Unemployment, and Hayek." *Federal Reserve Board of St. Louis Bulletin* (May 1975): 10.

Spooner, C. *The International Economy and Monetary Movements in France 1493–1725.* Cambridge: Harvard University Press, 1972.

————. *Risk at Sea: Amsterdam Insurance and Maritime Europe 1766–1780.* Cambridge: Cambridge University Press, 1981.

Stein, Herbert. "Pre-Revolutionary Fiscal Policy: The Regime of Herbert Hoover." In *The Fiscal Revolution in America.* Chicago: University of Chicago Press, 1969.

————. "An Empirical Analysis of the Debate over Rules versus Discretion with Special Reference to the Monetary Management of the German Bundesbank from 1958 to 1970." Ph.D. diss., Florida State University, March 1973.

Svennilson, Ingvar. *Growth and Stagnation in the European Economy.* Geneva: United Nations Economic Commission for Europe, 1954.

Tanner, J. Ernest, and Vittorio Bonomo. "Gold, Capital Flows, and Long Swings in American Business Activity." *Journal of Political Economy* (January/February 1968): 44–52.

Temin, Peter. *The Jacksonian Economy.* New York: Norton, 1969.

Thornton, A. P. *The Imperial Idea and Its Enemies: A Study in British Power.* New York: Auden Books, 1968.

Tobin, James. "The Monetary Interpretation of History." *American Economic Review* (June 1965): 464–485.

Triffin, Robert. *The Evaluation of the International Monetary System: Historical Reappraisal and Historical Perspectives.* Princeton: Princeton University Press, 1965.

Tucker, Donald P. "Bronfenbrenner on Monetary Rules: A Comment." *Journal of Political Economy* 71 (April 1963): 173–179.

U.S. Congress. House. Committee on Banking and Currency. *Compendium on Monetary Policy Guidelines and Federal Reserve Structure.* Pursuant to H.R. 11. Subcommittee on Domestic Finance of the Committee on Banking and Currency. House of Representatives. 90th Cong., 2d sess., 1968.

————. Committee on Banking and Currency. *Stabilization.* Hearings before Committee on Banking Currency. House of Representatives on H.R. 11806. 70th Cong., 1st sess., 1928. U.S. Congress. Joint Economic Committee. Standards for Guiding Monetary Action: Report of the Joint Economic Committee. Washington, D.C.: U.S. Government Printing Office, 1968.

————. *The Impact of the Federal Reserve System's Monetary Policies on the Nation's Economy.* Staff Report of the Subcommittee on Domestic Monetary Policy of the Committee on Banking, Finance, and Urban Affairs. 96th Cong., 2d sess. Washington, D.C.: U.S. Government Printing Office, 1980.

U.S. Congress. Senate. Committee on Banking and Currency. *Restoring and Maintaining the Average Purchasing Power of the Dollar.* Hearings before Committee on Banking and Currency. Senate. on H.R. 1 1499 and S. 4429. 72d Cong., 1st sess., 1932.

Viner, Jacob. *Studies in the Theory of International Trade.* New York: Harper and Brothers, 1937: 119–349.

————. "The Necessary and the Desirable Range of Discretion to Be Allowed to a Monetary Authority." In *In Search of a Monetary Constitution,* edited by L. B. Yeager. Cambridge, Mass.: Harvard University Press, 1962.

Vuchinich, W. S. "Interwar Yugoslavia." In *Contemporary Yugoslavia,* edited by W. S. Vuchinich. Berkeley: University of California Press, 1969.

Walker, Charles E. "Fact and Fiction in Central Banking." *Essays in Monetary Policy in Honor of Elmer Wood,* edited by P. C. Walker. Columbia, Mo.: University of Missouri Press, 1965.

Walsh, Carl E. *Monetary Theory and Policy.* Cambridge, Mass.: Massachusetts Institute of Technology, 1998.

Warburton, Clark. "The Volume of Money and the Price Level Between the World Wars." *Journal of Political Economy* 53 (June 1945): 150–163.

————. "The Secular Trend in Monetary Velocity." *Review of Economics and Statistics* 30 (March 1948): 128–134.

————. "The Misplaced Emphasis in Contemporary Business—Fluctuation Theory." *Journal of Business* 19 (October 1946): 199–200. Reprinted in *Readings in Monetary Theory.* Selected by a committee of the American Economic Association. Homewood, Ill.: Irwin, 1951.

————. "Variations in Economic Growth and Banking Developments in the U.S. from 1835 to 1885." *Journal of Economic History* (September 1958): 283–297.

Weintraub, Robert E. "Congressional Supervision of Monetary Policy." *Journal of Monetary Economics* (April 1978): 341–362.

Whittlesey, Charles R., and J. S. Wilson, eds. "Rules, Discretion, and Central Bankers." *Essays in Money and Banking in Honor of Richard S. Sayers.* London: Oxford University Press, 1968.

Wildavsky, Aaron. *The Politics of the Budgetary Process.* 2d ed. Boston: Little, Brown and Company, 1974.

Willett, T. D. "International Specie Flows and American Monetary Stability." *Journal of Economic History* (March 1968): 28–50.

Williams, David. "London and the 1931 Financial Crisis." *Economic History Review* (April 1963): 512–528.

Williamson, J. G. "International Trade and the U.S. Economic Development, 1927–1943." *Journal of Economic History* (September 1961): 372–380.

Wisely, William. *A Tool of Power: The Political History of Money.* New York: Wiley, 1977.

Yeager, Leland B., ed. *In Search of a Monetary Constitution.* Cambridge, Mass.: Harvard University Press, 1962.

———. *International Monetary Relations: Theory, History, and Policy.* Part 2. New York: Harper & Row, 1966.

Yohe, William. "The Intellectual Milieu at the Federal Reserve Board in the 1920s." Presented at the annual meeting of the History of Economics Society, Duke University, May 25, 1982.

Young, Allyn A. "Economics and War." *American Economic Review* (March 1926): 1–13.

Index

About the Author

GEORGE MACESICH is Professor of Economics at Florida State University. He is the author of many books, including, most recently, *World Economy at the Crossroads* (Praeger, 1997) and *Money, Systems, and Growth: A New Economic Order?* (Praeger, 1999).

ISBN 0-275-96777-8

9 780275 967772

HARDCOVER BAR CODE